Adventure into Science

Harry Thomas B.Sc., M.I.Biol.

Artist: Mike Jackson   Photographer: Philip James

Hamlyn
London · New York · Sydney · Toronto

Contents

　　Outside　　　　　　　　　　　　5
　　Inside　　　　　　　　　　　　　7
　　Getting Organised　　　　　　　8
　　Into Action　　　　　　　　　　9
　　On the Jelly Trail　　　　　　　10
　　A Well-set Gel　　　　　　　　12
　　All-round Diffusion　　　　　　13
★　A Colourful Experience　　　　14
★　In the Steps of King Alfred　　16
★　More Burning Questions　　　18
★　Enter Nitrogen　　　　　　　　20
　　Demolition　　　　　　　　　　22
★　White Powder Detective　　　23
　　Test your own Enzyme　　　　24
★　A Cautionary Tale . . .　　　　25
★　A Cautionary Tale 2　　　　　26
　　Nearing the End
　　　　of the Jelly Trail　　　　　27
　　Agar Micro Garden　　　　　　28
★　More about Colour　　　　　　29
　　Adding and Subtracting Colour　30
★　Fizz　　　　　　　　　　　　　32
　　The Refrigerator　　　　　　　33
★　Ways of Preserving　　　　　　34
　　Taming a Fungus　　　　　　　35
　　Models　　　　　　　　　　　　36
　　Hunt the Carpel　　　　　　　　37
　　A Lucky Interlude　　　　　　　38
　　A Pictorial Interlude　　　　　　39
　　How does your Garden Grow?　40
　　A Window-sill Mini Zoo　　　　42
　　Further Tasks　　　　　　　　　44
　　Onwards　　　　　　　　　　　45

★　**These experiments require an older person to be present**

Outside

Left: trees are grown in plantations to provide timber for planks and beams, and for pulping to make paper. We usually see only the finished products **below** in a house.

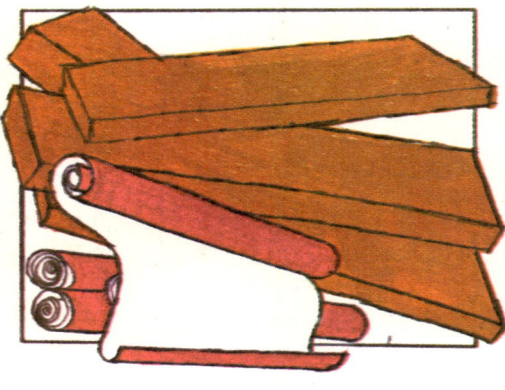

Left: clay is dug out and shaped into moulds, and then baked. The bricks **below** can last for hundreds of years. What is the oldest brick building known to you?

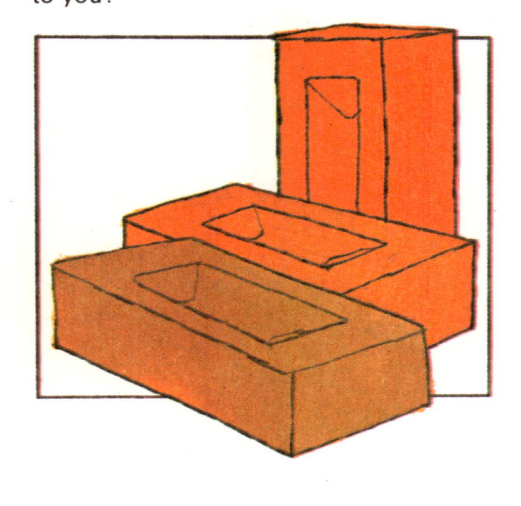

In making cement tiles **left** the cement is mixed with materials which give it the colour required. It is easier to *make* units all the same size and shape **below** than to choose pieces of natural material which are as uniform. The applied science used in making things is a branch of TECHNOLOGY.

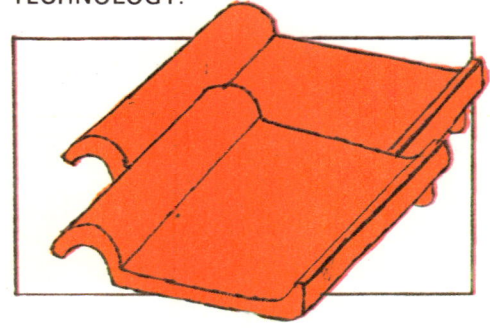

Most of you who read this book will live, as I do, in some sort of house. What is meant by 'living' in a house? It means doing many everyday, familiar things, such as eating, sleeping, relaxing and getting on with hobbies and interests in leisure time. It also means working — keeping the house clean and in good order, decorating, cooking and so on. The house gives us shelter within which to live, so that we can protect ourselves from sun, wind, rain and snow. The interior of the house can be made warmer by some sort of heating system, or made cooler by various means.

Most of this we take for granted. I want to suggest to you in this book that there are many interesting things in and about a house that we can use to help us understand science and how scientists work.

I hope that you will find that 'investigating' the objects and materials about the house can be an enjoyable hobby, and add to the list of leisure activities that keep you happy at home.

Houses differ a good deal from one another, and some of the features of my house will not apply to yours, and yours will contain things that mine does not. I do not think this matters, for I hope that after reading the book you will want to go on to investigate all sorts of problems that I may not even mention here. So when I talk about my house, and some of the things I have found interesting to study in it, I am merely offering you some samples of the kind of thing that may be done.

I live in quite an ordinary house, in an ordinary street in South London. The house was built about seventy years ago. It is the end of a row of terrace houses. Its walls are made of bricks and mortar. Originally the roof was covered with slates, but two years ago I had these replaced by cement tiles. The floors and rafters are made of wood. The internal walls are lined with plaster, and covered with paint or wallpaper.

This is not very exciting information, so let us see what is to be said about these materials so far. They all come from mineral or vegetable sources. Bricks are made from clay which has been baked. In this process particles of clay are melted into one another to give a waterproof, insoluble mass. In its original state the clay readily mixes with water to form mud. The particles of aluminium silicate in natural clay are very small.

Slate is also made from clay! But clay is turned into slate by great pressure under the earth, over many, many centuries. The pressure makes any flat particles in the clay line up so that the slate eventually formed can be split along these lines. We have hard rocks made from soft in each case, but one is formed quickly by heat applied by human action, and the other is formed very slowly by natural pressure.

A chemical process goes into the making of mortar, which is a mixture of lime and water. Sand and ashes may be added as 'filler' material. The lime is calcium hydroxide, and this slowly hardens to calcium carbonate by action of the gas carbon dioxide in the air. Calcium carbonate is also found in the natural rock, limestone.

But this is mostly about the outside of the house.

Let's go inside!

The dynamo **above** produces electric current by moving conductor coils between magnets.

The barometer **below** measures air pressure, which is important in relation to weather.

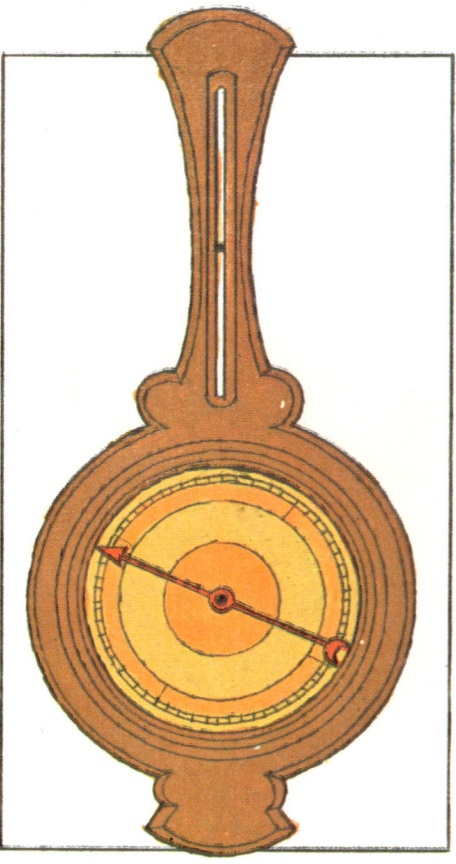

Much of our coal comes from seams deep in the earth, and special gear **above left** is needed to lift it to ground level, and to enable miners to descend the pits to work the seams.

Some gas for light and heat still comes from coal, from which it is driven off by heat. However, here **left** we see a rig used to extract 'natural' gas from beneath the sea.

Inside

We step into the hall, which has paper on the walls, and rugs on the floor. There is a hall stand, some bookcases and some pictures on the wall. We could discuss the science behind paper making, and the origin and nature of the material in the rugs. We could also consider the science behind a barometer, hanging up further along the hall. And so we could move through the whole house, writing up a mass of scientific knowledge — that other people had found out. But as I have said, our purpose here is to use the house and things in it to experience something of the way a scientist sets about finding things out. So we will let the illustrations remind us of the 'already known' science, and now go on to concentrate attention on things which show promise in the way of investigation.

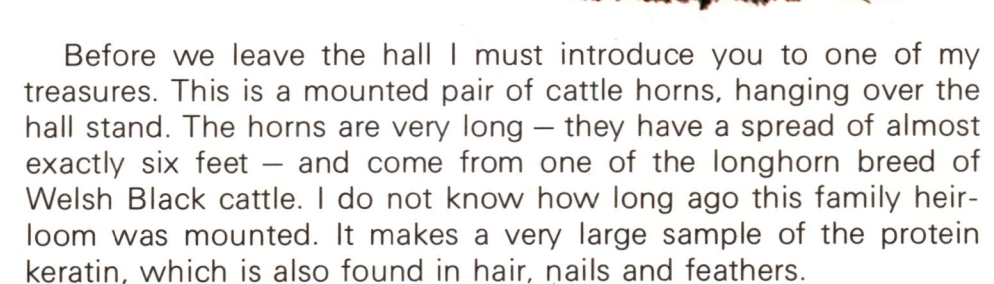

Before we leave the hall I must introduce you to one of my treasures. This is a mounted pair of cattle horns, hanging over the hall stand. The horns are very long — they have a spread of almost exactly six feet — and come from one of the longhorn breed of Welsh Black cattle. I do not know how long ago this family heirloom was mounted. It makes a very large sample of the protein keratin, which is also found in hair, nails and feathers.

The kitchen is going to be our most useful department, I feel sure. Just consider these items, all white or colourless solids, in the 'dry' cupboard: table sugar (=cane or beet sugar = sucrose), glucose, starch, gelatine (for making jelly), agar (another jelly maker), kaolin (china clay), citric acid (= lemon flavouring), tartaric acid (used in baking), bicarbonate of soda (=sodium bicarbonate, also used in baking), salt (sodium chloride), soda (=sodium carbonate, washing soda), vitamin C (=ascorbic acid), 'health salt'. . . . There should be scope for investigation there.

Also in the kitchen there is a variety of jams, marmalade and jelly ready for making up with water 'following the instructions'. Then there is vinegar — brown malt vinegar, and white wine vinegar — each mainly acetic acid, in water. In the handyman cupboard, there is methylated spirit, 'white spirit' and medicinal paraffin. Not all of these are drinkable (and when in doubt assume it isn't). I think we can now make a practical start.

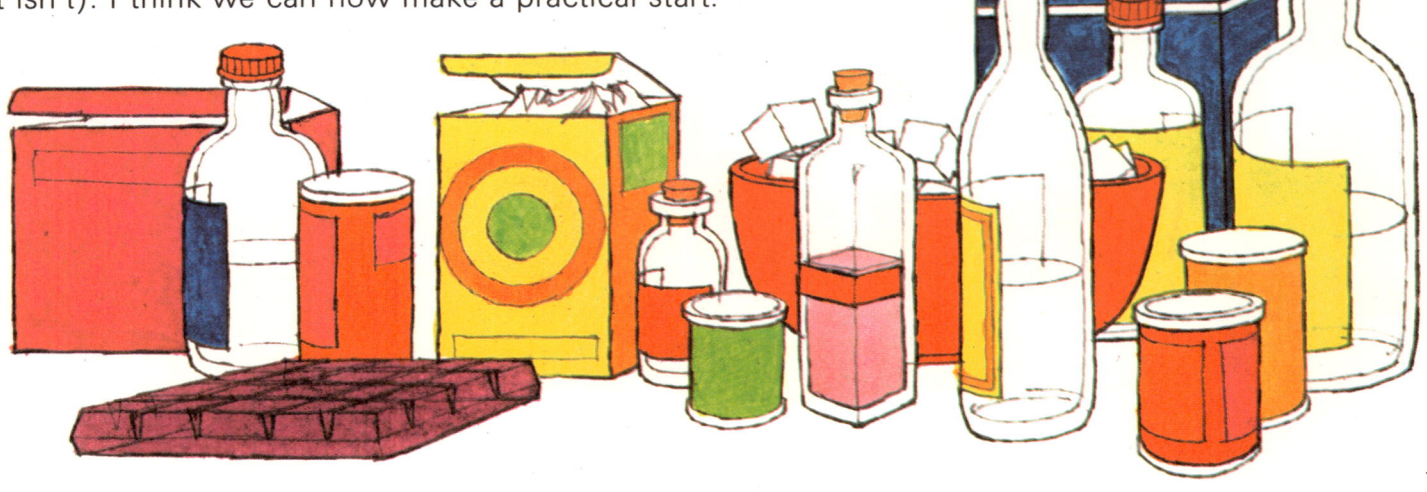

Getting Organised

In suggesting some lines of investigation that can be carried out at home, I have tried to use only materials and equipment that you could expect to find in an ordinary house. This is not a book on how to set up a home laboratory, with special laboratory equipment, though that would be an interesting thing to do. It is a book about trying to be scientific with limited resources.

But we must have tools to work with, and you may have first to collect together a number of the items I suggest, no doubt with the help of your friends. So here is my basic catalogue of useful items: jam jars, and larger jars; plastic, metal and glass cylindrical tubes (and their caps or stoppers); drinking 'straws', especially those made of transparent plastic; clear plastic cheese boxes, or the lids in some cases (very useful, these); white blotting paper; various plastic trays and cups; metal cans with one end removed (useful for standing tubes in, especially); metal, and clear transparent, kitchen foil.

You will need somewhere to keep these items, clean and in orderly fashion ready for instant use. If you can keep the units of an experiment together in one box or on one tray you can set it aside neatly in a safe place until you have finished with it. You will need working space. If you are lucky and can have the use of a room or even a table of your own, make the most of it. But I did a great deal with trays and a shelf.

If what you are to do is to be proper science, you will need to label and record your work. The illustrations and notes on following pages will give you some ideas on how this may be done. But there is no reason why you should not work out methods to suit yourself.

You will, of course, also need to take full safety precautions in what you do. This is not only to avoid accidents and damage, but in order to make sure that the experiments you carry out are to do what you want them to do. Thus, for instance, you must use clean apparatus, and not get materials mixed up — unless the experiment requires it. You will need to work with clean hands, so as not to transfer traces of materials on your fingers to the wrong places. Washing your hands and clearing up after you is not only good policy to get co-operation from the rest of the family, but part of the routine behaviour of a good scientist.

These familiar items **above** take on a new role as scientific apparatus as we carry out our 'research'.

Left: this is the way to use a drinking straw as a pipette. Put your thumb over the upper end, dip the straw in the liquid, and lift your thumb. Liquid runs into the straw, and when you seal the upper end again with your thumb, stays there when you lift the straw out. Move the straw (and contained liquid) over to the vessel you want to put it in, and lift your thumb again. The liquid now runs out into the vessel. This is a neat method, and you can see exactly how much liquid you are transferring.

It is a good idea to wear a pinafore or an overall. Make sure you wipe down the kitchen bench after use.

Into Action

An investigation often starts when one notices something interesting or unusual, which in turn makes one ask a question. If the question cannot be answered by someone who might be expected to know the answer, or the answer cannot be found in a book, perhaps a well thought out experiment will enable one to find out. Here is an example.

The other day, when I was helping with the washing up, I rinsed out the dark purple juice from a dish that had been used to hold some canned black cherries. The sink had just been cleaned, and given a 'freshener' with some washing soda. As some of the juice mixed with traces of the soda, it changed to a blue colour. Why did the colour change? That was the observation, and the question. I happened to know that soda behaves as an alkali, and that some dyes have a different coloration in contact with alkali from what they show when in contact with acid, or when 'neutral'. You may have heard of, or even used, litmus paper, which is red with acid, blue with alkali, and purple when neutral. Was the cherry juice a similar material, and a possible home version of litmus?

This suggested the first experiment. I decided to take a number of coloured juices, and some of the dyes used as food colours, and to examine them in neutral, acid and alkaline conditions.

The washing soda was not the strongest of alkalis, but it was safer than caustic soda, of which I had none at the time. Caustic soda is used in some oven cleaners. I chose acetic acid as my acid, in the form of the colourless wine vinegar. It is a rather weak acid, and I could just as well have used citric, tartaric or even ascorbic acid.

Among the items I had collected from local shops as possibly useful apparatus was a piece of polystyrene pressed into the shape shown in the picture. Having tested it first for leaks, and finding it sound, I used it to make a neat array of tests, as you can see. I am not sure that the colours in the illustration are *exactly* as I found them. Here is a case where you will no doubt want to check for yourself. This is good scientific practice. Anything a scientist claims to do must be able to be repeated by another if it is to be accepted. So careful repetition of experiments is part of the job. But you may also wish to extend the experiment, using other juices and colours, under yet further conditions.

It is interesting to note that some of the artificial food colourings did not change, but in most instances all natural colours do alter.

So we found that not only cherry juice, but several other juices, could be used as acid/alkali indicators. How this is so is a rather complicated story, needing advanced knowledge. Solving one problem often brings up others in science. In this book we will find quite a number of problems and attempt to solve some of them. There will not be space to try to solve them all, or even mention some problems that might arise. But so long as you get some idea of the way in which one can try to tackle problems by observation and experiment, and in the end are interested and confident enough to try for yourself, you will have made proper use of the book.

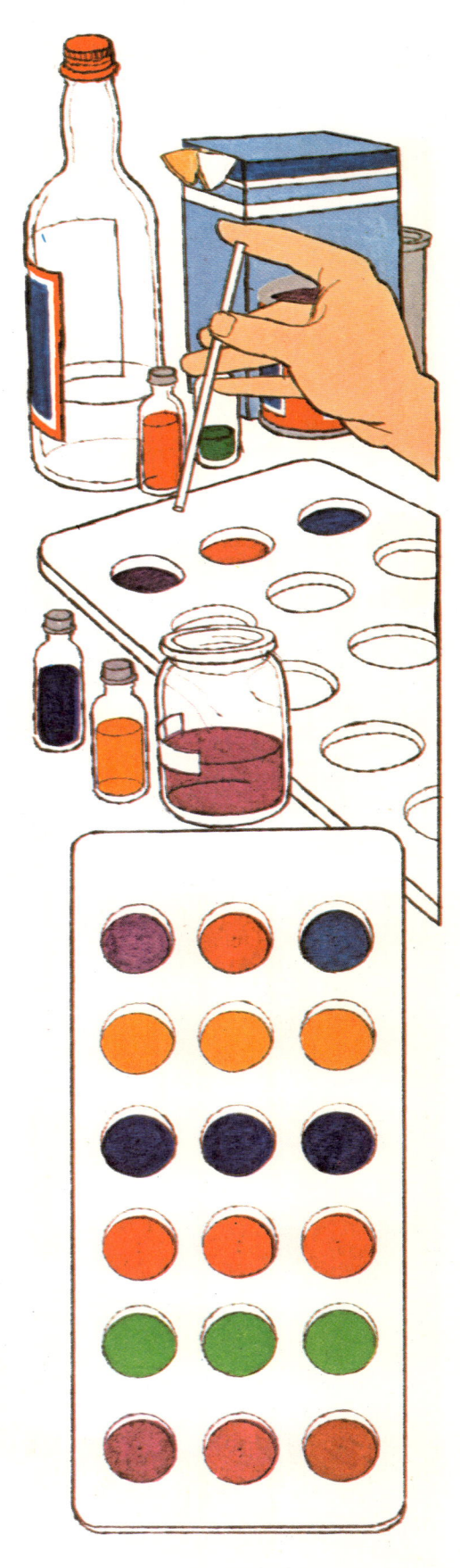

The left column **above** is the unaltered juice. Acid was added to the middle column, and soda to the one on the right. The coloured materials, reading from top to bottom are black cherry, yellow food colour, blue food colour, cochineal food colour, green food colour and beetroot juice.

> HERE WE GO ON A VOYAGE OF DISCOVERY WITHOUT LEAVING THE KITCHEN.

On the Jelly Trail

One of the disadvantages of working with liquids is that they easily spill, even if you are careful. It occurred to me that I could avoid this in the colour investigation if I used jelly. A jelly is made from a gelatine preparation, just by adding hot water, so the larger part of jelly must be made up of water.

I made up a 'blackcurrant' jelly from a packet so labelled. The colour looked as if it should be very much like the black cherry juice. I rescued some of the jelly from the tea table, and poured it into several of the plastic cheese lids and let it set. I then put a spot of the white vinegar (acetic acid solution), and some soda solution, onto the jelly. To my surprise, there was no colour change, at least at first, and only an orange tinge under the soda after a long wait.

The granules of gelatine here are being thoroughly stirred with hot water to make sure it all dissolves.

Fruit juice is mixed with the cooled jelly to give a colour not too weak, not too strong.

The still liquid jelly is poured into the plastic lid container and left to set.

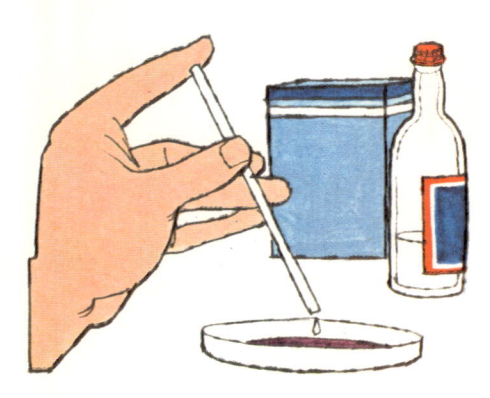

A drop of acid or alkali is carefully placed on the set jelly using the drinking straw pipette.

Here **right** you see the red spot where acid was added, and the blue spot made by soda.

I had assumed that the purple colour of the 'blackcurrant jelly' was genuine blackcurrant colouring. But, either I was wrong to suppose that I could work with jelly rather than with watery juice, or the colour was artificial.

I decided I must make up some jelly from colourless gelatine, and add some juice from a jar of blackcurrant jam, or from freshly stewed blackcurrants. The latter would have been better, but for convenience I used the jam. When the purplish jelly set, I put drops of vinegar and soda solution on as before, and this time in a short while a more definite red appeared under the acid, and a bluish colour under the soda. It looked as though the jelly method would do.

The colour changes were not so well marked as those with the cherry juice (and the label on the jam jar admitted the use of colouring matter in addition to the fruit itself) so I made up, with gelatine, a supply of black cherry jelly to use as my main material.

Using this, I found that acid gave a bright red colour, and the soda a quite deep blue-grey which developed a light brown zone in the centre. But next morning, the red colour had *spread beyond the boundaries of the drop of acid* and the blue-grey zone had spread outside the soda region. This meant that the acid and alkali had drifted or DIFFUSED through the water contained in the jelly. I then tried blobs of ink, food colour and a few other materials, and found that they slowly diffused outward too.

This observation made a starting point for a further study. If I were to use a *colourless* gelatine jelly I should be able to observe the diffusion more clearly. I prepared some colourless jelly by heating some water in a cup in a saucepan of water, and stirred in some of the small granules of gelatine from the packet. I guessed what I thought would be a suitable amount of gelatine. The jelly set all right when it cooled, but some new questions arose. How much water can be mixed with gelatine and still give a jelly which sets? In what circumstances does jelly set most easily?

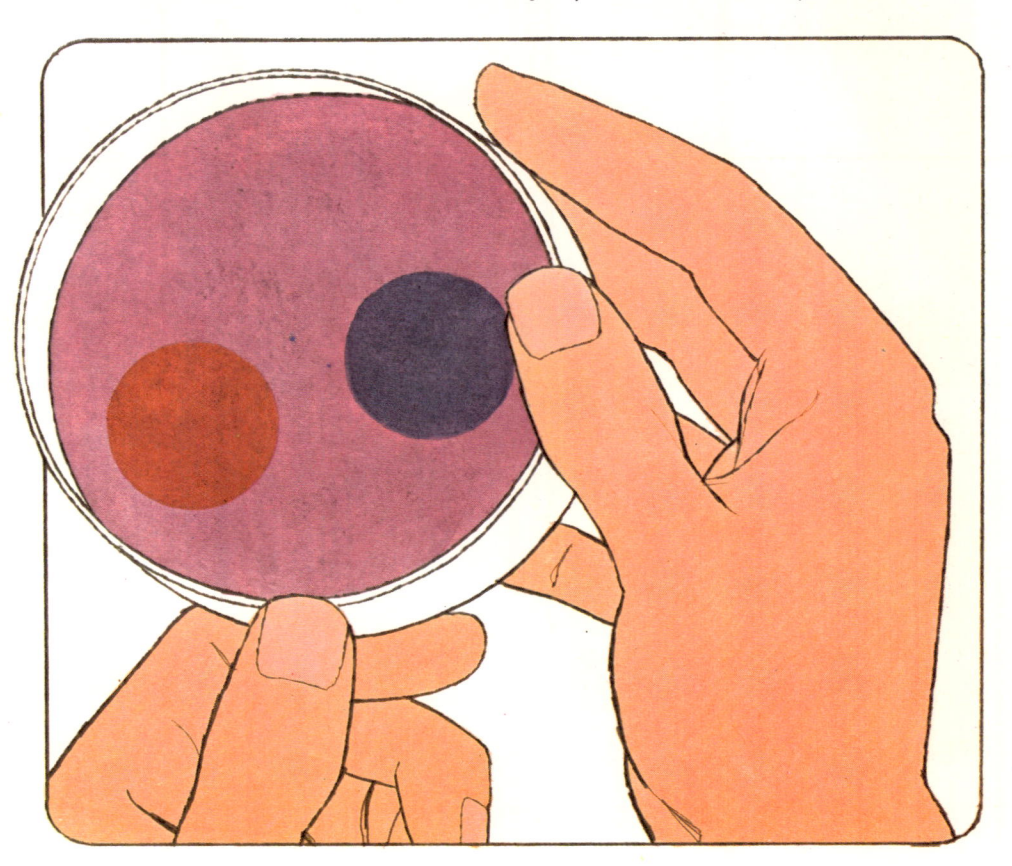

A Well-set Gel

The gelatine jelly I had prepared set quite stiffly, but of course, it was quite easy to melt by standing its container in hot water.

I took a standard amount of melted jelly by using a 5ml. plastic 'dose' spoon that had come from the chemist with some medicine on one occasion. This 'standard 5ml. unit' was put into each of eight tubes. Two of the tubes were not further treated, but into the others, taking them in pairs, I put 5ml., 10ml. and 25ml. of plain water. I labelled the tubes.

I left one set of tubes on a shelf in the kitchen, and put the other set in the refrigerator. I then inspected the tubes at about twenty-minute intervals. On the first inspection the undiluted jelly had set in the refrigerator. This, and the results of later inspections, are shown in the pictures.

We can conclude that the bigger the amount of gelatine in relation to water, the more readily the jelly will set. Also, setting is encouraged by a low temperature. Since all the jellies set in the end, we see that the refrigerator is useful for getting jellies to set quickly, and such jellies will stay set when brought out into a normal room. I expect you can see how I could have carried on this experiment, to find a strength of jelly which would perhaps melt when brought out of the refrigerator.

Why does a jelly set at all? This is beyond home science, but what we have seen fits the explanation that materials which gel have long units or molecules which can stick together to form a 'scaffolding' within which water is held. Molecules move about, the more rapidly the hotter they are. The molecules of gelatine move less, and hold together more easily, when cool.

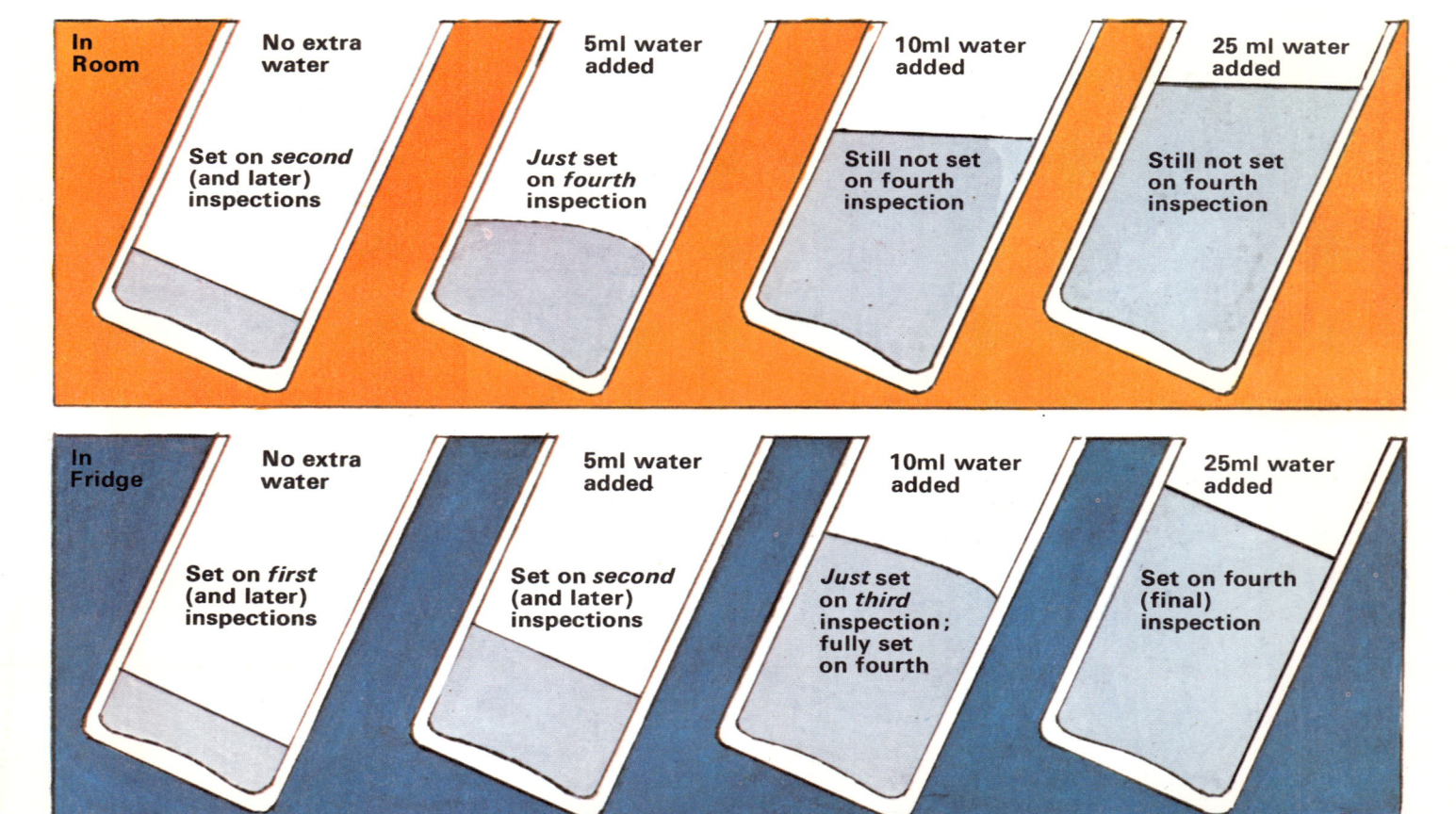

The long protein molecules of gelatine **above** move separately in the unset jelly, but **below** link to a network when set.

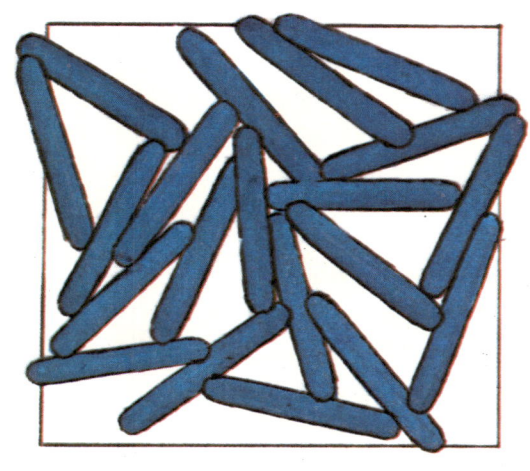

Below: the effect the temperature had on the setting is shown here — in warm room **top** and in refrigerator **bottom**.

In Room	No extra water	5ml water added	10ml water added	25 ml water added
	Set on *second* (and later) inspections	*Just* set on *fourth* inspection	Still not set on fourth inspection	Still not set on fourth inspection

In Fridge	No extra water	5ml water added	10ml water added	25ml water added
	Set on *first* (and later) inspections	Set on *second* (and later) inspections	*Just* set on *third* inspection; fully set on fourth	Set on fourth (final) inspection

All-round Diffusion

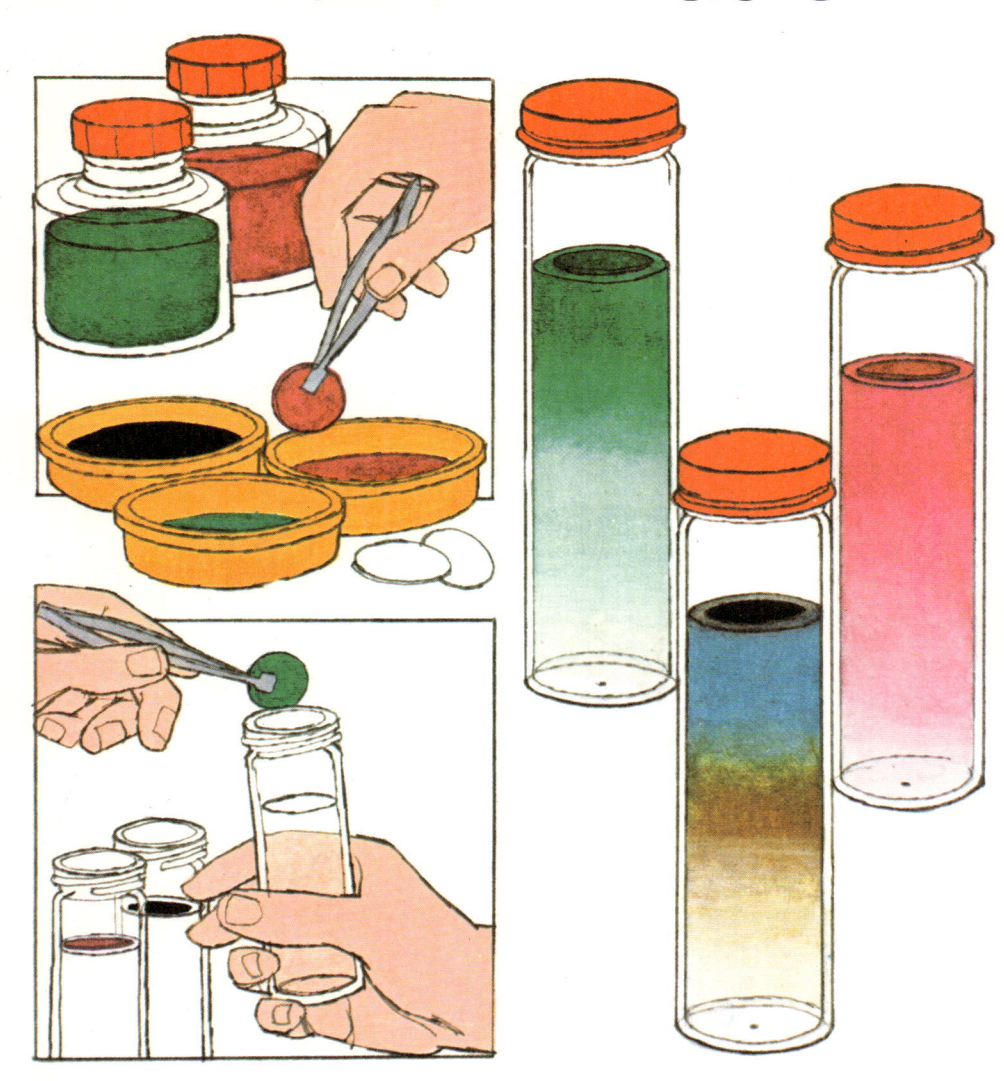

Far left: discs of blotting paper are being dipped into coloured inks. The discs are then **lower far left** carefully placed on top of set gelatine in tubes. The larger picture just to the left shows the appearance of the tubes 'right way up' after about a day, and the picture below shows how just the same colour pattern has occurred with tubes which were immediately turned upsidedown. The diffusion has occurred just as well upward as downward. The tiny units (molecules) of colour move at random in all directions.

I wondered, when colours spread out in jelly, whether they only spread horizontally. To test this, I put some clear jelly in several tubes and when it was set, I put some discs of blotting paper, that had been soaked in various coloured materials, on top. You can see from the illustrations that the colours spread down through the jelly, but not always at the same rate, and in the case of the black manuscript ink, a brown colour went far into the jelly, and a blue colour only a little way.

But perhaps this experiment only shows that colours 'fall' down through the jelly. To find out if this were so, I tried the same experiment, with discs of the black ink from a felt-tip pen, and the black manuscript ink, but this time, after sticking the discs on the jelly, *immediately* turned the tubes upside down, and kept them that way. As you can see, there is no noticeable difference between these and the tubes kept right way up. So it looks as though materials that will dissolve in water can spread out, or diffuse, in all directions.

But another question must be asked. *Is* the diffusion through the water, or the gelatine? Can we find other materials which can gel? There is a material called AGAR, which comes from a Japanese seaweed, which is used in cooking and confectionery, which can be made up just like gelatine, and a rather pasty gel can be made from starch. I found diffusion took place in a similar way in agar and starch gels, and the thing they have in common is the water.

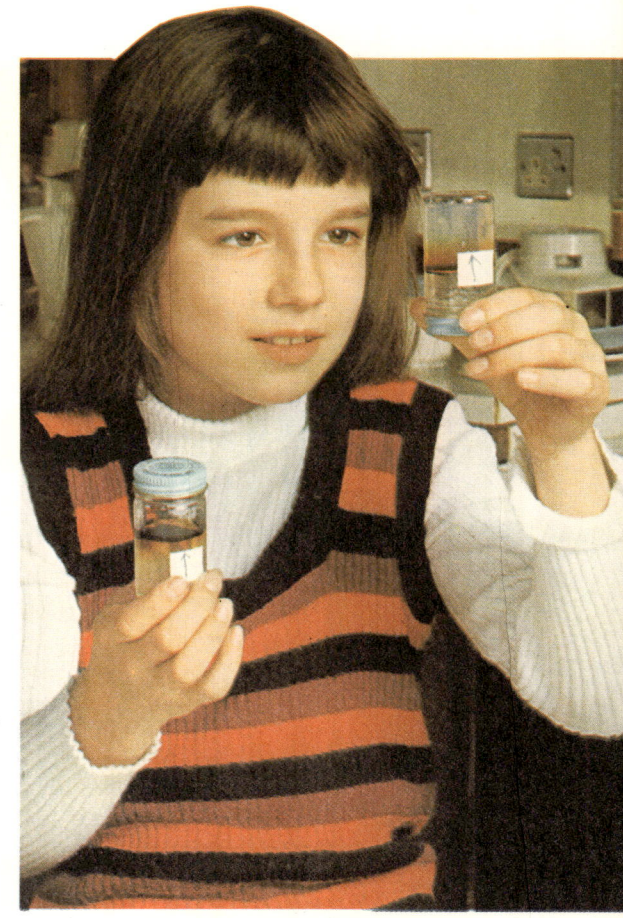

13

★ A Colourful Experience

In the diffusion experiments I had used only one coloured material in each case, though it looks as though some of them, such as the black ink, are really mixtures. But suppose two different diffusing materials meet? Do they interfere with one another, or go on independently?

In order to test this, I used blue and yellow food colours, neither of which had behaved like a mixture. A small blob of each colour was put on top of the jelly. In fact I tried it on gelatine, agar and starch gels. Results were similar in each case. The picture is of the gelatine example. The circles of blue and yellow spread out steadily, but where they overlap there appears the single colour green! This perhaps reminds you of the way in which you can mix blue and yellow paints to make green.

Why not try other colour mixtures, and see whether you find your experience with paints from a paintbox agrees with what you find from diffusing colours.

At this point we come up against one of the problems that face scientists. So far, the items we have dealt with have led from one to the other. We now have, in the questions about colour, another line to follow before we have finished with the jellies. Starting with one investigation often leads to several unexpected new questions, and each of these can lead to still others. So we will have to come back to colour later.

It looks as if colours just mix together as they diffuse into one another. But what about materials meeting that might *act* on one another? Though the acid and the soda are colourless, so that one cannot see them diffusing, perhaps something happens when they meet. Indeed, a few bubbles appear in the jelly *between* the blobs of acid and soda after a while. I found this effect was seen more strongly if I made little pits in the jelly, into which I put solid tartaric acid and solid *bi*carbonate of soda. Quite a distinct row of bubbles appeared. This means some kind of chemical reaction had occurred. We talk more about this later in the chapter on Fizz.

This experiment was done with gelatine jelly. With agar jelly I got bubbles much less readily. But gelatine is 'stretchy' and allows bubbles of gas to form. The more 'brittle' agar would let gas escape, rather than stretch.

However, I tried a further experiment to see how a liquid bleach in jelly would behave towards green felt tip ink. It quickly bleaches this ink when applied directly. This time, the bleach fizzed as soon as it contacted the gelatine jelly, and melted a hole in it! But when I put bleach on agar jelly there was no reaction, and the experiment with the green ink went as shown in the picture. You can see how far the (invisible) bleach has travelled by the decolorised zone in the diffusing green ink. Agar *is* the suitable gel for this experiment. There is more to come about jellies, but I want first to go on to something else. You could say I am going to make a fresh start, but you will see that jelly will prove to be a useful material in the new investigation.

TAKE GREAT CARE WHEN USING BLEACH AND KEEP IT FROM YOUR EYES AND MOUTH. WEAR RUBBER (OR PLASTIC) GLOVES, RINSE SPLASHES WITH PLENTY OF WATER.

On the right we are comparing the mixing of paints from a paintbox with the diffusion mixing of colours in jelly (see picture below). Colours which are useful for giving other colours when mixed, are in some way mixed themselves! (See pages 29–31) The 'blue' paint or food colour must somehow have green in it, and so must the yellow. (Why not make a colour-mixing chart?).

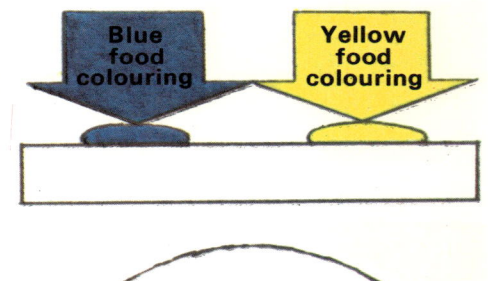

Here we see how blue and yellow food colours diffusing through gelatine jelly appear as green where they overlap one another.

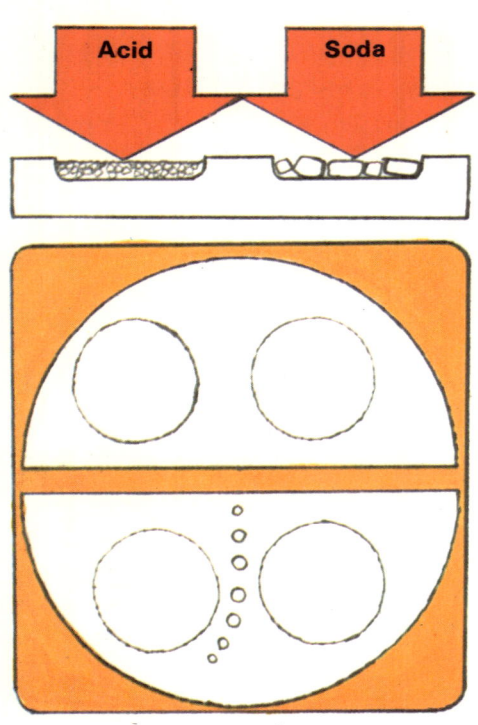

Colourless acid and colourless soda cannot be *seen* diffusing through colourless jelly, but the row of bubbles shows where they must have met one another.

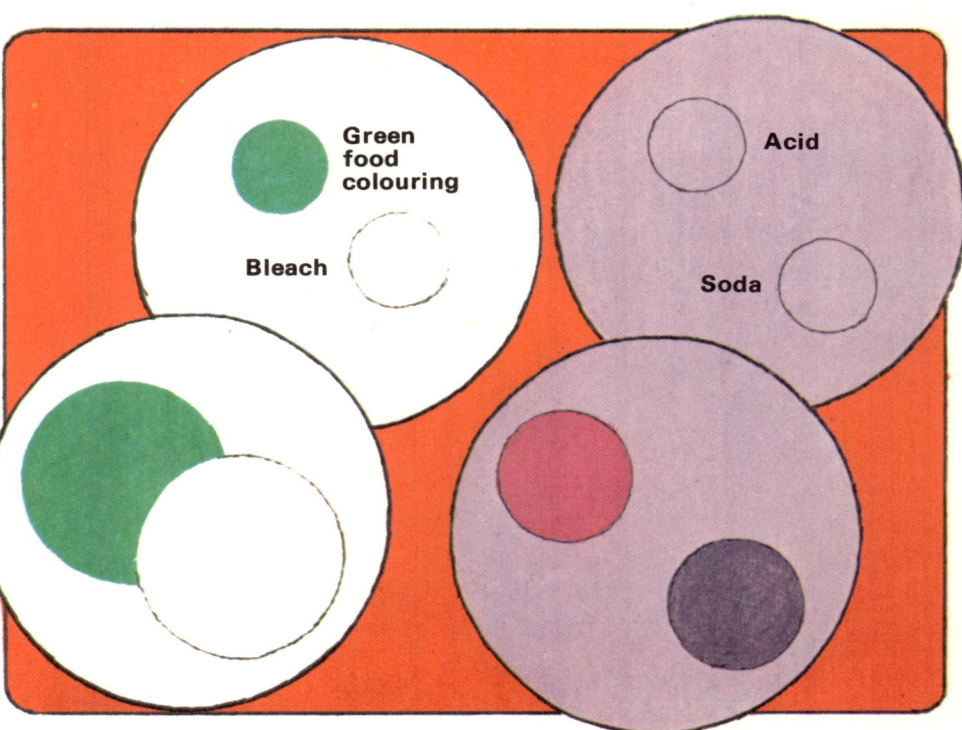

We cannot see bleach diffusing through the colourless agar, but the 'bite' out of the diffusing green circle shows where the 'bleach front' is.

How does the colour difference here compare with the cherry juice colours? Why not test a whole range of purple juices in this way?

15

★In the Steps of King Alfred

Making charcoal

I was in disgrace the other morning. I'm afraid I burned the toast. It didn't really help when I explained that I hadn't really burned it, but only charred it. It would have been in flames if it were really burning. . . .

What had happened to the toast? The carbohydrate starch which is the main chemical ingredient in the bread, changes chemically on heating, in a complicated way. The tasty, crisp brown material is formed in an early stage of heating, but if heated for too long, or with too hot a source of heat, the starch really breaks down into the chemical element carbon, and water in the smoke that comes off. Water is made from hydrogen and oxygen. (There is a clue here about the name 'carbohydrate'.)

Of course, carbon itself will burn. Coal is mainly carbon, and charcoal is an impure form of carbon. But in order to burn, oxygen is needed. We can make charcoal if suitable material containing combined carbon is heated out of contact with air. If you have a coal fire, or make bonfires in the autumn, you can enclose some pieces of wood in a tin can with a lid, with a *few small* holes punched in it, and set it in the fire and leave it until the latter goes out. This gives you wood charcoal. You can make animal charcoal if you do the same thing with some pieces of bone instead of wood.

How long does a piece of toast take to cook? In this experiment, slices of bread are put under the grill for half a minute, or one minute, or one and a half minutes, etc. You can see some results on the plate. Why not find the 'true toasting time' for your grill?

Washing and drying charcoal

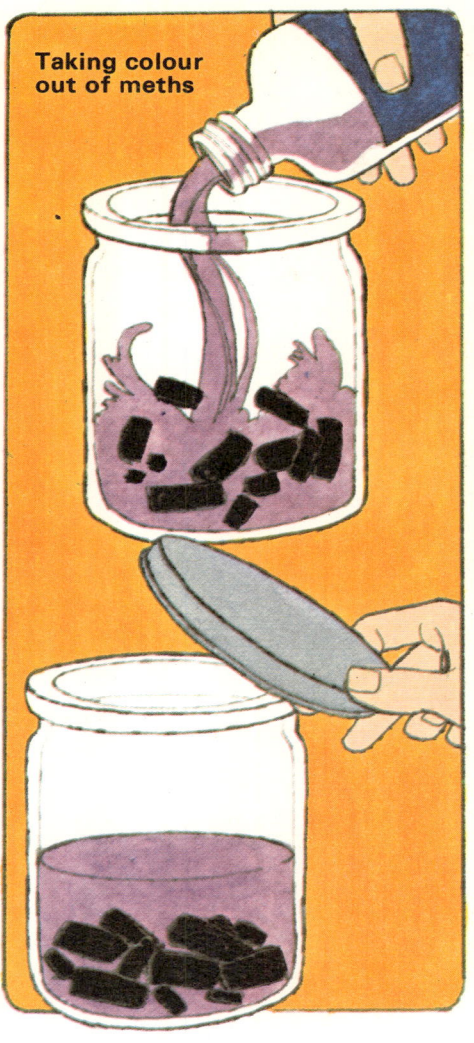

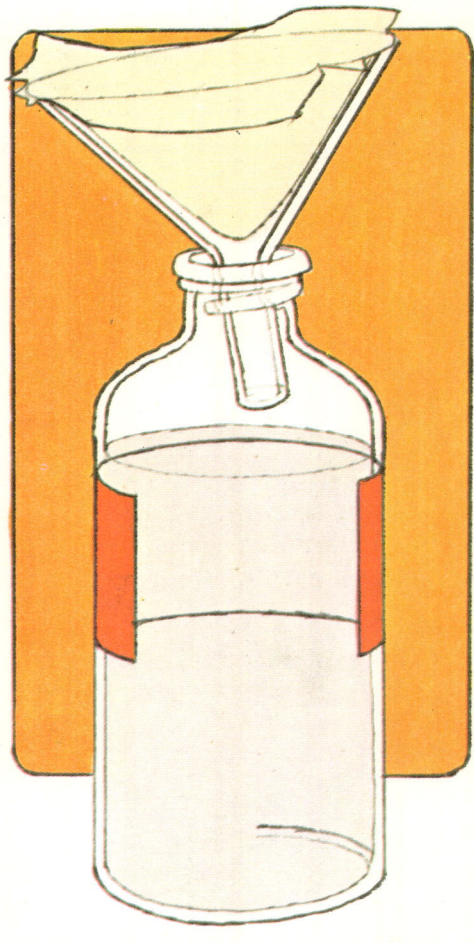

Taking colour out of meths

Filtering meths into storage bottle to keep out bits of charcoal

These two kinds of charcoal have the power to *absorb* certain materials. Plant charcoal absorbs gases. It is used in respirators for this purpose. Animal charcoal absorbs many coloured dyes and other coloured material. We can make use of this.

'Methylated Spirit' as usually bought is a purplish liquid and having a foul taste. The main ingredients are ethyl and methyl alcohol. These are poisonous. So a substance known as pyridine, with a dreadful taste is added deliberately to make it undrinkable. A violet dye is added so that you can also *see* a warning — for otherwise the methylated spirit is as colourless as water. In fact 'industrial' and 'surgical' spirit are sold without the colour added. But they are not so easy to get and are more expensive. We shall need some colourless spirit later, so I include instructions on decolorising the methylated spirit.

Wash your prepared animal charcoal with several rinses of water, and put to dry in a cool oven, in a tray. When thoroughly dried, allow it to cool, and put some in a clean jar. Pour some methylated spirit over the charcoal, and leave for a while. Put a lid on the jar, for the spirit easily evaporates, and is a fire risk if care is not taken. You should find that most if not all of the colour will be taken up by the charcoal. Strain or filter off the decolorised methylated spirit, and keep it in a well-stoppered bottle or can. You *must* label this clearly with something like 'Decolorised meth — solvent only'. The colourless methylated spirit may *look* like water, but it is poisonous and inflammable. Since, as we shall see, inks may dissolve in methylated spirit, a 'lead' (graphite) pencil is best for labelling.

BE SURE TO LABEL YOUR METHS CLEARLY. RINSE SPLASHES WITH PLENTY OF WATER.

★ More Burning Questions

The mention of bonfires gives me an excuse to say a few words about flames and burning. A gas flame seems to stay still, but is really a steady flow of invisible unburnt gas entering a hot reaction zone — which is the flame. (See the Bunsen burner below.) In a candle flame, there is a very slow downward movement of the flame as the heat melts the wax, which creeps up the wick as oil, and then vapourises. The vapour partly burns, and partly forms carbon particles which become white hot, but show up as soot in the smoke which rises beyond the burning zone. In an explosion, a flame spreads so rapidly through the burnable materials as to produce great heat and noisy expansion. This may be very dangerous but is harnessed in a car engine.

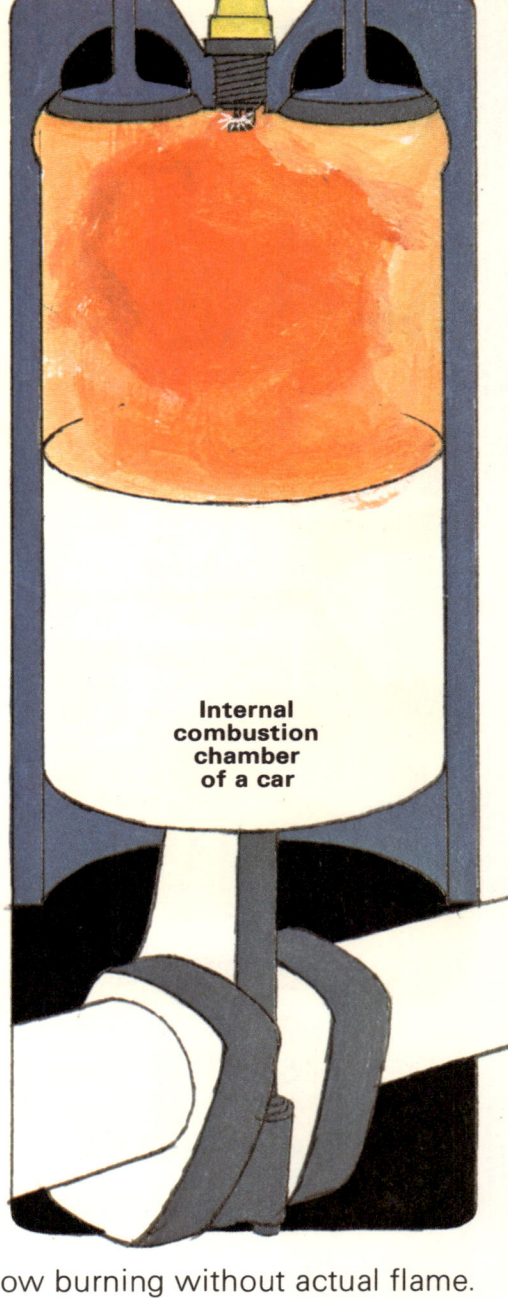

Internal combustion chamber of a car

This is the string-char-glow-ash pattern. It is **worth** experimenting with different sorts and thicknesses of string to find which one best keeps on glowing slowly and steadily. Remember to dip string in water after use to extinguish.

In smouldering string we get slow burning without actual flame. As it smoulders note how the heat of the smouldering spot chars the next bit of string, before it is burned away itself. When the red spot has moved along there is left a strand of ash, i.e. the mineral material in the plant fibre from which the string was made. The smoke that comes from charring and burning actually contains water vapour. It is not very easy to prove this at home, but the smoke will *just* deposit a trace of mist on a mirror in the same way as the water vapour in your breath does when you breathe on it. A mirror cooled in a refrigerator works best.

The charring is a sign of carbon, and the fact that water comes from *burning dry* string means that at least hydrogen must be present in some form in the string.

The ash, of course, cannot burn. It is what is left after burning. Keep this point in mind.

If something has charred, it contained carbon. Most materials which come from living things, plant or animal, may be expected to contain carbon. Would you expect this to be true of the foods that animals eat? If so, would you expect to find that foods char on heating? This suggests a line of experiments — but we need to be mindful of safety when heating things.

Here a young friend shows how to use matches sensibly. She has closed the box after taking a match out, struck the match away from her, and unhurriedly lit the candle.

Above & top: it makes a great difference whether you have the arrangement flame/foil/paper or flame/paper/foil. You cannot be too careful with fire and flame!

We can, in fact, do an experiment which gives us clues about safety. Spread a sheet of paper on a flat surface, and place a layer of metal foil on top. Strike a match and put it, still alight, in the centre of the foil. Let it burn out. Then lift the foil and examine the paper underneath. Is it charred? Now place a *small* piece of paper on *top* of the foil, and this time put a lighted match on the paper. What happens in this case?

Do you agree that (a) we should take care not to leave easily burned material just lying around when doing heating experiments, and (b) a sheet of metal foil makes a good safe surface on which to do heating work?

You will see other hints about heating experiments on this page. When you are testing materials use small quantities, as little as you can. It is quicker, safer and less wasteful. Scientists scornfully accuse people who use needlessly large quantities of material in experiments of doing 'bucket analysis'!

Sometimes there may only be small quantities of a substance available, so it is important to be able to work with small amounts. Even if you have plenty of material, it is wise to use small samples, to ensure that you have enough to repeat experiments or carry out new ones.

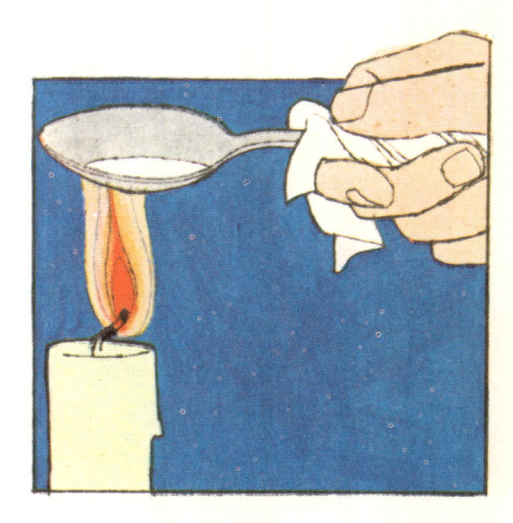

This is to remind you that if you use metal, such as a spoon, to heat, you need an 'insulating' handle, such as a damp cloth.

★ Enter Nitrogen

CAREFUL WITH AMMONIA! DON'T LET IT GET NEAR YOUR EYES AND TAKE CARE NOT TO SNIFF TOO HARD. IF SPLASHED RINSE WITH WATER.

Among the materials that charred when I heated them were gelatine and agar. There was no particular smell to be noticed when the agar was heated, but the gelatine smelled rather strongly. I noticed a similar smell when I heated feathers, and nail clippings.

Did you know that in bygone days people used the fumes from burning feathers to revive someone who had fainted? Today we use smelling salts. Some smelling salts contain ammonia (a compound of nitrogen and hydrogen) which has a 'wakening' effect when sniffed. Some cleaning materials contain ammonia — it usually says so on the label — which you can smell very clearly when you warm some gently. BUT DO BE CAREFUL!

Here is a test for ammonia, which has its smell mixed with others in heated gelatine, etc. A strip of blotting paper soaked in black cherry juice, and partly dried off so that it is only moist, then held over ammonia to absorb the gas, will change colour. Try this yourself, and note the change. This is a useful test for ammonia, for it is the only vapour you are likely to come across which does this.

What happens when you hold your cherry test paper in the vapour or fumes from the gelatine? You can see from the picture what I found. The same thing happened when I used the paper to test heated feathers. No doubt it is the ammonia in heated feathers that acts as the reviver. The ammonia given off by the heated gelatine means that the latter contains nitrogen and hydrogen as well as the carbon seen on charring.

When I tested the vapour coming off agar, I got no such colour change. It looks as though agar may not contain any nitrogen.

These tests fit in with the information that gelatine is a protein, containing carbon, hydrogen, nitrogen and oxygen, but that agar is a carbohydrate containing carbon, hydrogen and oxygen only.

The jar contains ammonia in solution; some of the gas is coming off and affecting the moist cherry-paper.

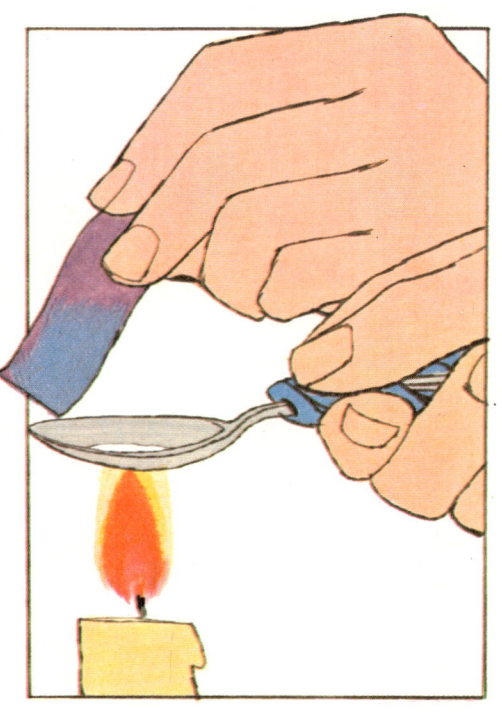

Heated gelatine fumes are also turning the paper blue. (Cherry-paper *must be quite moist* to resist burning).

Do this *quickly* — moist paper ready, and into the fumes as soon as they appear — to reduce smell!

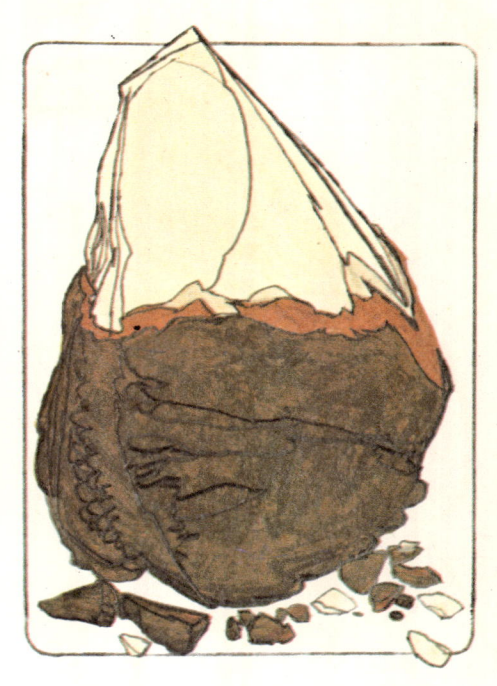

If the Brazil nut is sharpened to a point and stood on end (whether or not completely removed from the shell), it can be lit with a match and will burn for several minutes.

Far left & left: the match will not light the corner of a sugar cube, unless some ash (see page 18) is first added. It will burn long enough for the flame to set paper alight.

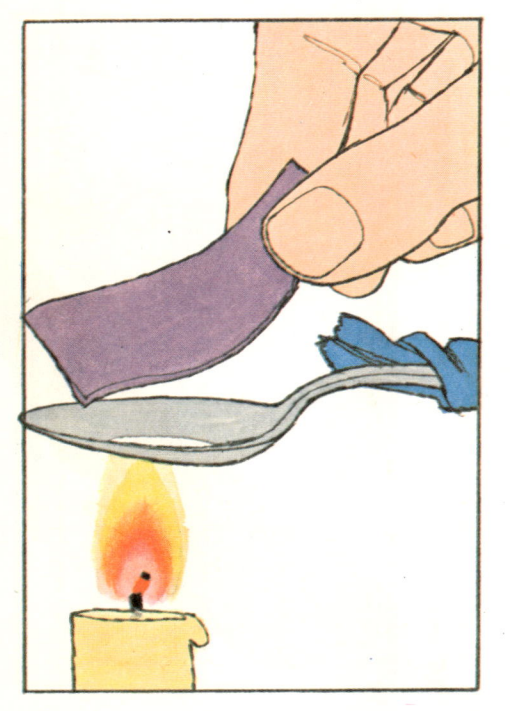

When the agar was heated, the fumes did not make the colour change found in the rest.

Foods contain carbon, which in the form of coal, coke or charcoal we know to be fuel material. Could our foods be fuel of some sort? Take a lump of sugar as an example. Try to set it alight by bringing a match flame to one corner. I expect you are as unsuccessful as I always am! But if you put a little ash (such as from smouldering string) on a corner, you may succeed, as I usually do, in getting a small flame going, which burns for a little while. So the sugar is a fuel, but in the experiment burns only in the presence of ash. You remember this ash itself cannot burn. The ash, in fact, is here acting as a CATALYST. This is something that allows or encourages a chemical reaction to take place, but remaining unchanged itself.

If instead of a lump of sugar you take a Brazil nut (or other sort of nut?) and cut it as in the picture, you can get this to light directly, and stay alight for quite a while. The sugar is 100% carbohydrate, but though the nut contains materials other than fat (or oil), it burns the more easily. Fat is a better fuel than carbohydrate.

But in our bodies we do not burn our foods with flames! How do we get the energy from them? The ash gives the clue. There are special catalysts called ENZYMES in our bodies, which allow changes such as a kind of burning, to take place very gently. We shall have more to say about enzymes.

21

Demolition

It is not only in burning our foods for their energy that our bodies make use of enzymes. Some foods, like the proteins such as gelatine and starch, need to be broken down before our bodies can use them. The units, or molecules that make up these materials are large, but are built of smaller units. These are amino acids in proteins, and glucose in starch. This breaking down of the larger units into the smaller is called digestion. The enzymes which help in digestion are specialists. An enzyme which will digest a protein would not digest starch, nor would a starch-digesting enzyme break down proteins.

We can do some experiments to test this statement. Prepare two dishes of clear jelly, one of gelatine, the other of agar. Onto each put a small pinch of an ordinary powder detergent, and of a so-called Biological Washing Powder. The latter is supposed to contain an enzyme which 'removes difficult stain like egg, gravy and blood'. These contain proteins. If this is a true claim, we would expect to find the gelatine dissolved away under the 'biological' powder, but not the ordinary detergent.

The agar should not be dissolved by either. (Many substances added to jelly may soften it a little — for reasons too complicated for this book — so do not be misled. Look for a great hole in the jelly.)

As you see, I found a hole in gelatine under the biological detergent, but not the ordinary sort. Neither made a hole in the agar.

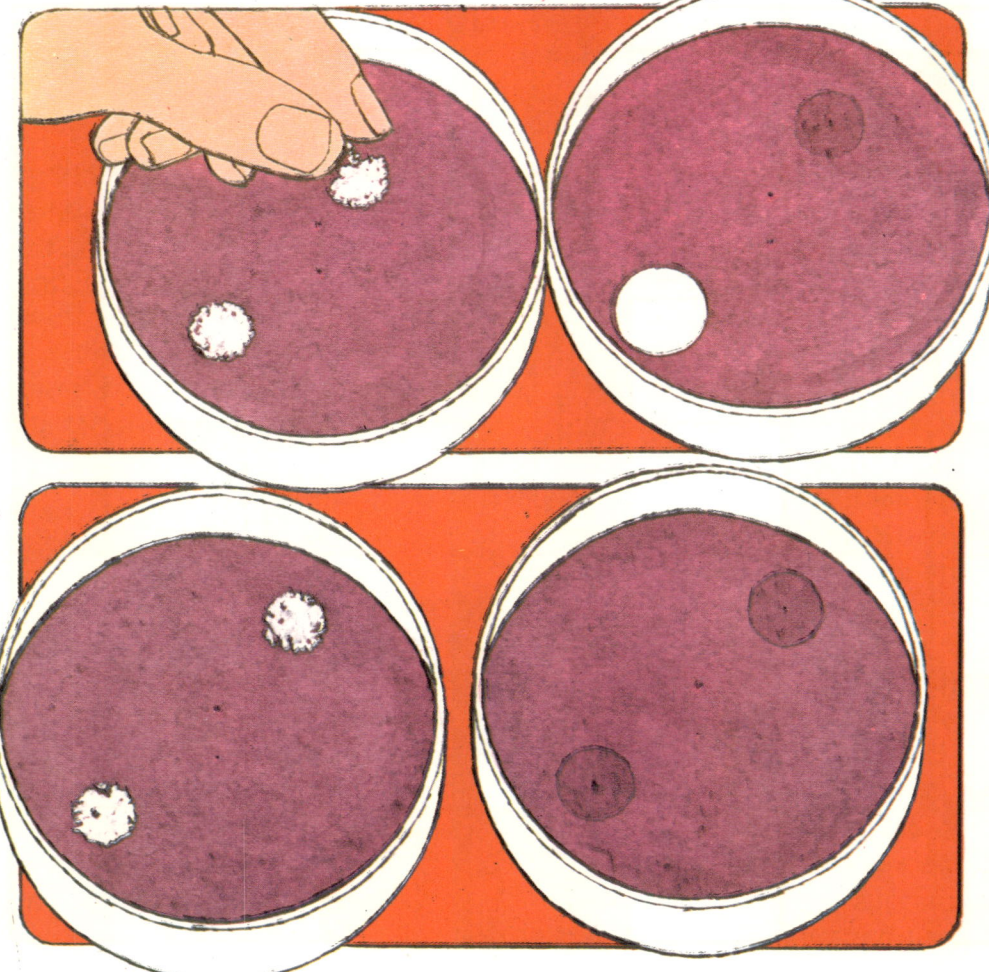

Far left: the start of the experiment; result just to the left. The upper experiment is the gelatine trial; the agar trial is below. In each dish, ordinary detergent on the upper right, 'biological' detergent on the lower left.

Above: two standard eggs were boiled together, and two identical yolk-stained spoons left! The one in ordinary detergent still has yolk on it, but yolk has been digested from the one in 'biological' detergent.

White Powder Detective

We have seen that we can distinguish between gelatine powder and agar powder by heating and testing the vapour with our coloured paper, or by the biological detergent method. Now there are a number of other white (or near white) powders in my kitchen cupboards. I chose a selection of them to work out some tests on the basis of which I might be able to identify an unlabelled powder. The ones I chose were starch, glucose sugar, kaolin (china clay), sodium bicarbonate, salt, gelatine and agar.

The tests I used were (a) gentle heating followed by stronger heating, (b) use of cherry-juice paper for fume check for ammonia, (c) shaking with cold water in a tube, (d) mixing with boiling water, (e) adding vinegar (acetic acid) to the powder in a saucer, (f) adding iodine solution and (g) using a solution of the powder (if it dissolved) as part of an electric circuit.

You can see from the table that some things behave alike for some tests, but that for *these* tests on *these* powders, each powder has a *list* of results peculiar to itself. Agar does very little, and kaolin does nothing. (With a sufficiently hot oven we could make porcelain from a kaolin paste, dried out.)

You will later see that I have chosen some of these tests for special reasons. But in the meantime, how could you do further tests, on still more powders?

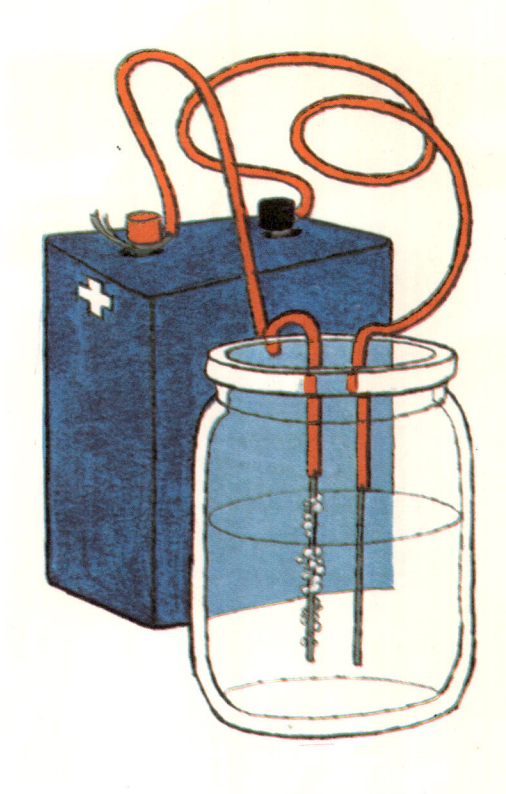

A 4½ volt battery is a suitable source of electric current for this work. Never try to use the mains – it is far too dangerous, and in any case it is alternating current, which is not used for such experiments. The wires should not be too far apart in the solution – the picture is about right – but they should not be allowed to touch, as this simply runs down the battery very rapidly. You might find it useful to rig up a stand to hold the wires steady.

	Starch	Glucose	Kaolin	Sodium Bicarb.	Salt	Gelatine	Agar
a	chars fumes burns	melts chars fumes burns	no change	no change	no change	chars fumes burns	chars fumes burns
b	no change	no change	—	—	—	turns paper blue	no change
c	no change	dissolves	no change	dissolves	dissolves	no change	no change
d	dissolves to thick paste	dissolves more easily	no change	dissolves more easily	dissolves more easily	forms clear gel	forms clear gel
e	no change	no change	no change	fizzes	no change	no change	no change
f	turns blue	no change	no change	no change	no change	no change	no change
g	—	no change	—	gas forms at negative electrode	gas forms at negative electrode	no change	no change

Test your own Enzyme

Though we started off with gelatine as the most familiar jelly-making material, it is not as useful for many purposes as agar. This carbohydrate material, obtained from Japanese seaweed, happens to be very hard to digest — very few living things can produce the enzyme able to do this. So a slab of agar jelly is, for all practical purposes, just a convenient way of having a non-spill, non-splash piece of still water! The agar is an inert support.

If you prepare an agar jelly, with which you mix a little 'starch solution' (see instructions), and when it is cold but not yet set, stir in also a small amount of iodine solution, you then have a tray of blue jelly. You have iodine-labelled starch spread through the jelly. Now collect a little of your own saliva, by taking a small sip of water, rinsing it round your mouth and spitting into a cup. Take just a drop of this saliva, and place it carefully on the starch-iodine-agar plate. Note the size of the drop. Inspect the plate at intervals. A slowly spreading colourless zone starting from the saliva drop shows that a diffusing enzyme is digesting the starch — turning it into something other than starch, that no longer goes blue with iodine.

Instead of, or as well as saliva, you could take a pea from a pod, and cut it in two, placing the cut surface in contact with the blue jelly. A similar clear, spreading zone shows that a plant, too, may have a starch-digesting enzyme.

The enzyme in saliva is a starch-digesting specialist. Saliva has no effect on the protein gelatine, nor on that other carbohydrate called agar.

To make starch solution mix a spoonful of starch with a little cold water in a cup **top**, to make a paste, then stir in boiling water. You may have to stand the cup in a saucepan of boiling water **above** and stir for a while to get a *clear* solution.

THERE ARE MANY ENZYMES IN YOUR BODY – ONE OF THE EASIEST TO GET HOLD OF IS IN YOUR SALIVA.

On the left of the picture is half of a pea, and a drop of saliva on the blue iodine-starch agar, at the start of the experiment. On the right: the result.

⭐ A Cautionary Tale...

Though I did not give the electric current test to the agar and gelatine jellies when doing the white powder tests, I decided to see the effect of an electric current on a jelly made up from black cherry juice. I knew there were a number of differences likely at the + and − electrodes, which might well produce colour changes. And so it proved. Within minutes there was a colour pattern rather like that in the picture when I used a 4½-volt battery as power supply. I was not surprised to find a jelly coloured with cherry juice conducting a current, for plant juices contain mineral salts in solution.

The colour changes happened so quickly that I thought this might be quite a sensitive way to detect current. Any two different metals in contact with any solution of acid, alkali or mineral salt ought to produce *some* current. If you are unfortunate enough to have needed fillings to your teeth, you may have noticed a peculiar taste if a piece of metal foil (tin or aluminium) comes into contact with the silver/mercury alloy of a filling. The slight amount of salt in your saliva, and these different metals, give a slight current which produces the taste. But it is not very convenient to connect your mouth by wire conductors to a jelly, perhaps for hours!

However, I knew that the citric acid in a lemon could be used, with copper and zinc stuck in the lemon, to give a weak current. I had some copper and steel (iron) wire handy and decided to be rather lazy, and set up a circuit as in the picture.... After about half an hour there was a colour difference around each of the wires in the jelly. Not very well marked, yet definite. But....

The scrap of metal foil acts as one of the electrodes, the filling in the tooth, the other. When the foil just touches, or is very close to the filling, and your tongue happens to get very close to this little 'cell', current affects the taste buds.

25

★A Cautionary Tale 2

... I decided I must check that the iron and copper alone had no effect on the jelly. So I cut half-inch pieces of each, washed them, and put them on the jelly. After half an hour there appeared the colour difference as before. If I had *not* made this check, I might have drawn quite the wrong conclusion.

I then set about doing the experiment properly. I found an old electric dry cell, and cut a strip of zinc from the casing. I hammered a piece of thick copper wire till it was quite flat, and cleaned it with emery paper. I stuck the zinc and copper into the lemon. As contact electrodes with the jelly I used aluminium foil. I first checked, of course, that this did not itself alter the colour of the jelly. I used clips to connect the zinc and copper to conductor wires, and clipped these to the foil. Half an hour passed. This time I found exactly the same colour changes as with the $4\frac{1}{2}$-volt battery.

So this jelly proved quite a delicate detector of current. I wonder if this idea will become famous as the cherry-flavoured electric lemon detector.

Using the $4\frac{1}{2}$-volt battery, I tested a jelly made up with juice from blackcurrant jam, and got similar, but less well marked results. But blackcurrant jelly made up from a packet reacted quite differently. There was a clear patch at the cathode electrode, but no change at the anode. This fits in with a much earlier observation.

Below: these pictures give you an idea of the results of the current-on-cherry-jelly experiment. The different response produced in the jelly by each electrode showed quite soon after the $4\frac{1}{2}$ volt circuit was set up (see top picture). The middle picture shows the similar result using the lemon-copper-zinc 'cell'. The bottom picture shows what I found with the 'packet' blackcurrant jelly and the $4\frac{1}{2}$ volt battery.

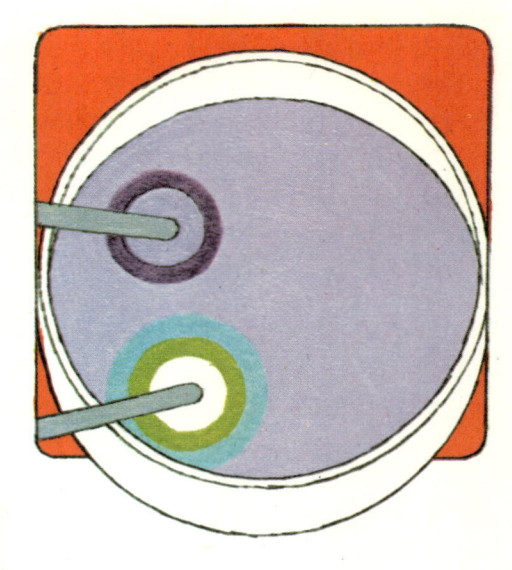

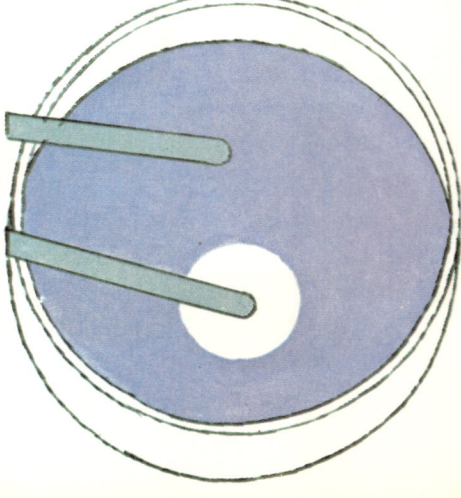

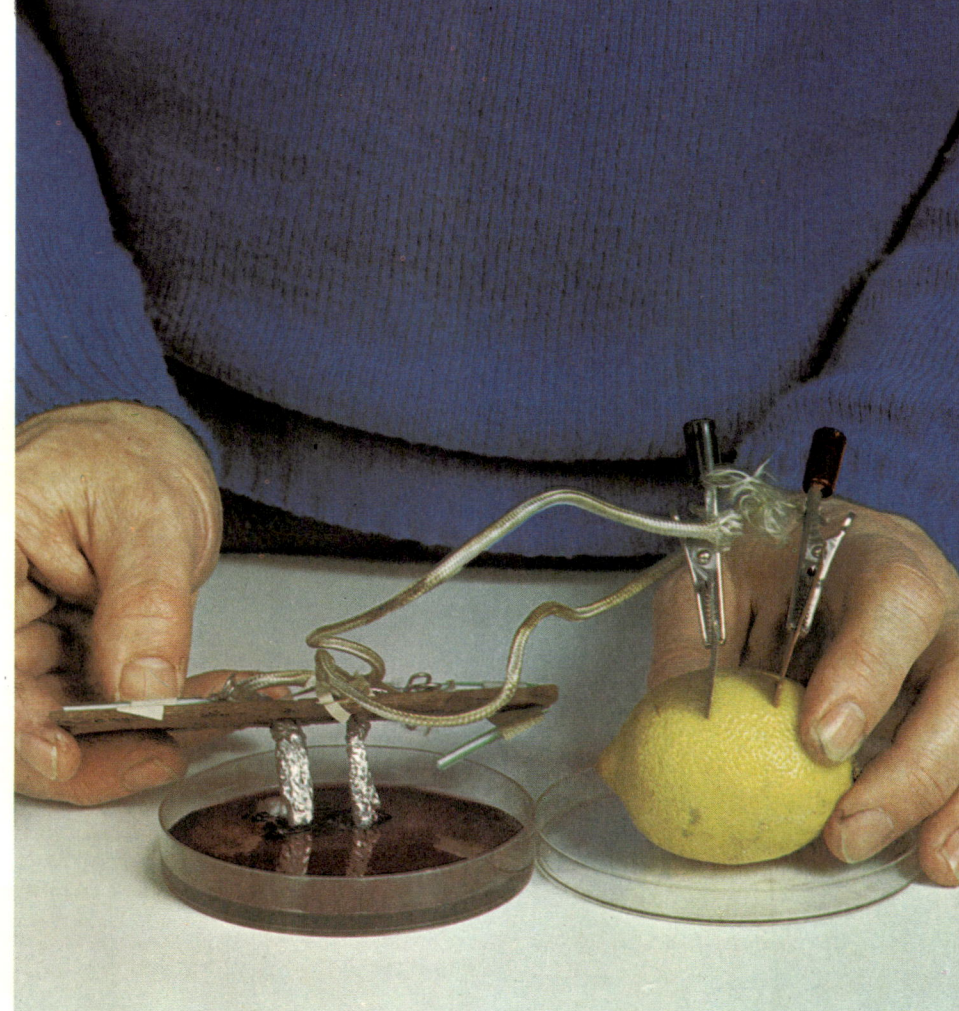

Nearing the End of the Jelly Trail

It would be quite easy to make the whole book about the study of jelly, but there are other things to interest us as well, so I want now to take leave of jelly study, by referring to some of the investigations that one might do, and some that I just started.

When I was trying out various materials on jelly before beginning the book, one of the things I put on some 'raspberry' jelly was a 50mgm. tablet of vitamin C (white in colour). After a while, a spreading zone of yellow replaced the red, and there was a brown ring round the yellow, as in the picture. But the jelly, according to the packet, contained gelatine, sugar, colouring and flavour. Which of these was being influenced by the vitamin C? I expect it was the colouring, and when I put a tablet on plain gelatine jelly there was no such colour, nor when sugar was added. So I suppose I would concentrate on colouring and flavour if I went on with this. How do you suppose such an investigation would develop?

The way jellies behave when they dry up would make another interesting study. Gelatine seems to take a very long time to dry out completely, and first form a very thick sticky layer. As a matter of fact, the original sort of glue *is* impure gelatine. Agar dries to a thin film rather like tissue paper, and with care can be peeled off its dish. You might be able to preserve some experiments in this way. There must be many more things to find out along these lines.

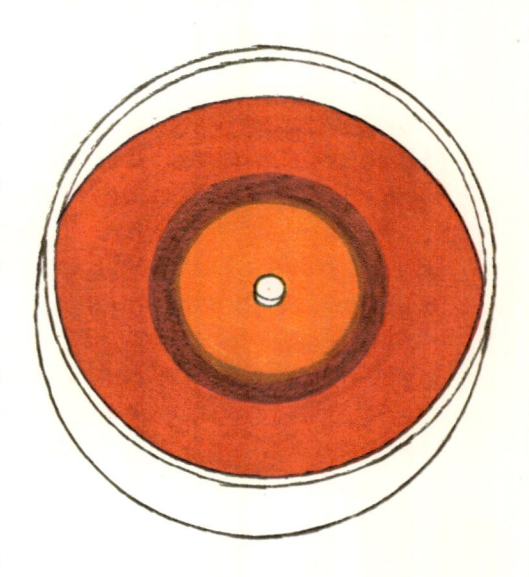

The mystery result: a yellow zone around a vitamin C tablet on raspberry jelly. My guess is that vitamin C bleaches the colour, but itself turns yellow as it diffuses.

Below left: fruit gums made from gelatine of animal origin. **Centre:** some of the little bits of coloured jelly sold as cake decoration have agar in them; one of the seaweeds from which it comes is shown. **Below:** the jelly in some pastilles is made from gum from the acacia tree.

Agar Micro Garden

There is one experiment, in which I use agar jelly, that I intend to work at long after the book is finished. I can now only report its beginning, but it does show how useful agar jelly can be.

Separating the unattached side of my house from the next one in the street is a passage-way which only gets the direct sun at midday. In this rather shady, and slightly damp place there grows a non-flowering plant, a liverwort, known as *Marchantia*. It has on its flat, scaley surface, some tiny cups, and in these there are very small grains, each no bigger than a full stop. Each of these is a gemma, and the gemma can quite easily be dislodged by raindrops, and be scattered rather like seeds, to start new plants.

The *Marchantia* plant is here shown enlarged, and a cup containing the gemmae is enlarged still further. To the right you can see the plate with gemmae set out on it, and the way in which one gemma grew is shown much enlarged to the right of that. The agar not only serves to keep the tiny plants in place, but because it is a jelly which contains much water, the *Marchantia* needs no watering.

I want to find out how these grow, and what conditions best suit them. So, as a first step, I have taken a tray of plain agar, and carefully planted out twenty-five gemmae, in five rows of five as in the picture. After four weeks, the gemmae have grown into what already look like tiny replicas of the parent plant. Now that I know they will grow on my agar, I can try a number of experiments, mixing different soils with the agar, giving different trays different amounts of light, keeping them in cooler and warmer places, and so on. I hope to find out enough to understand why it is *Marchantia* grows just where it does, and not just on any soil, anywhere. Though in a way this study belongs to the garden rather than the house, the agar method enables me to do the work indoors.

★ More about Colour

In some cases, coloured materials, such as the black ink, diffused in such a way as to show they might be mixtures of at least two substances. The effect was much the same in gelatine, agar and starch gels, and such separation as there was seemed to be due to slight differences in rate of diffusion through the water in the gels. Is there any way to get a better separation, and to analyse coloured mixtures into their components?

We can in fact do this quite easily by 'paper chromatography'. This makes use of the way in which blotting paper soaks up liquid. The pictures show how you can set up the experiment, and the results I obtained using water and methylated spirit as 'eluents'. (The method of picking materials up by the moving liquid is 'elution'.) The various colours tend to stick to the blotting paper to different extents, so the 'tug of war' between moving liquid and blotting paper lets the colours separate from one another. Notice that there is a difference between the patterns produced by the two liquids. They take part in quite different 'tug of war' contests!

A specially interesting case is the one where the original colour is the green matter of the leaf of a plant, just squashed onto the blotting paper. Hardly anything happens when water is the eluent, but spirit brings out bands of green and yellow. The green is chlorophyll, and the yellow made up of carotenoids. This latter colouring matter is concentrated in carrots.

Try out other colouring materials yourself. Which are single colours, and which are mixtures?

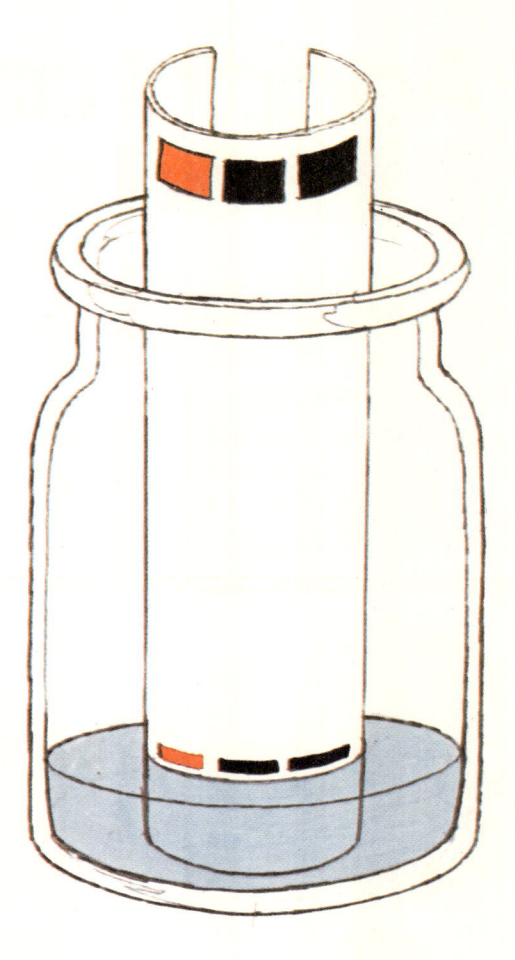

Above: the blotting paper stands in the liquid, with the ink to be analysed *just above* the level of the liquid. A patch of the original colour is put above each test line for reference.

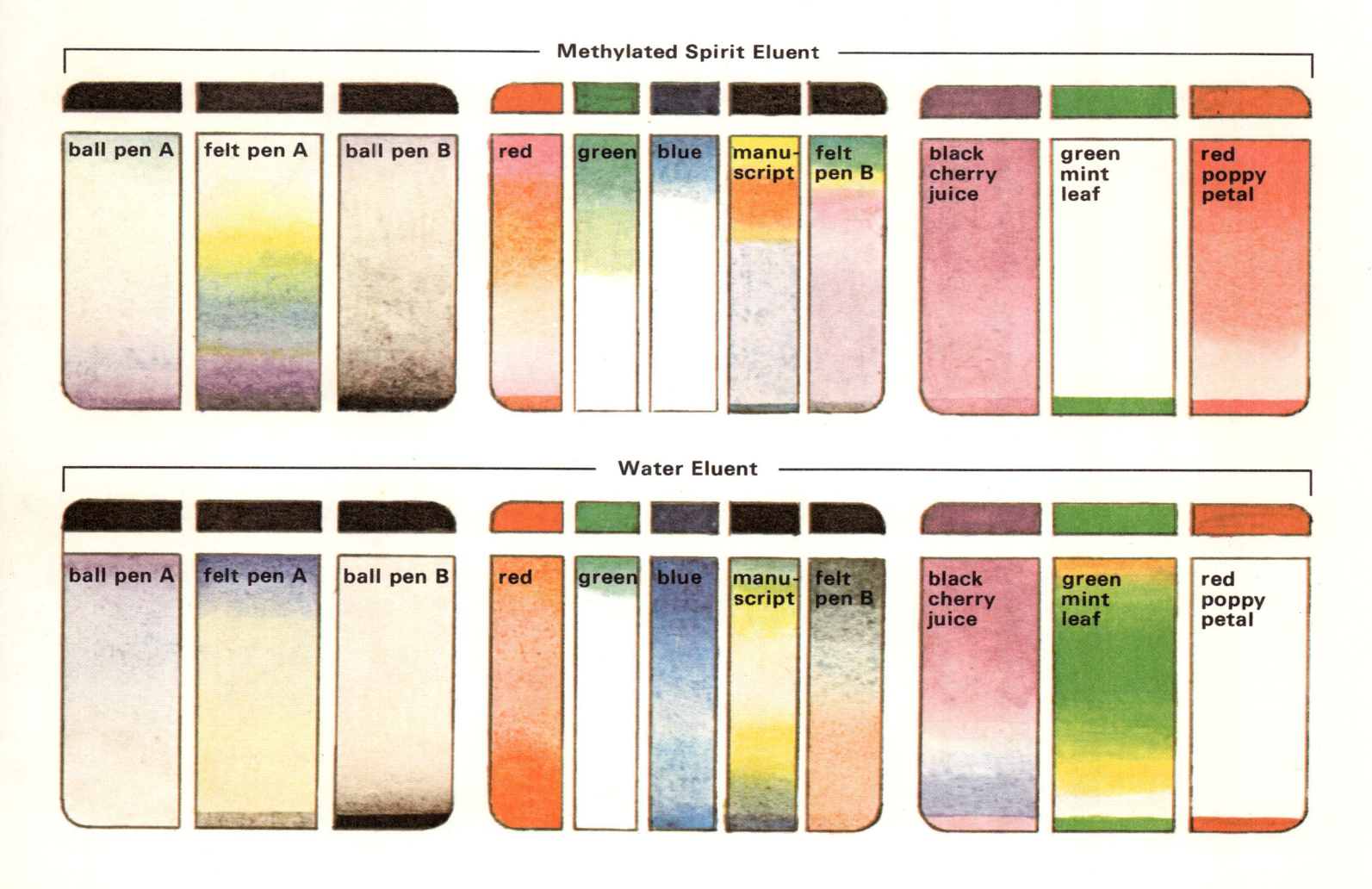

Methylated Spirit Eluent

| ball pen A | felt pen A | ball pen B | red | green | blue | manuscript | felt pen B | black cherry juice | green mint leaf | red poppy petal |

Water Eluent

| ball pen A | felt pen A | ball pen B | red | green | blue | manuscript | felt pen B | black cherry juice | green mint leaf | red poppy petal |

Adding and Subtracting Colour

One of the most interesting findings of the chromatography experiments is the fact that black inks are mixtures of colours — at least in some cases. I leave you to try Indian Ink, made from finely powdered carbon. What do you expect to find in this case? Now you will have noticed in the cases I analysed, that *different* mixtures of colours can make black. Why is this? To answer this we must make a fresh start.

Snow is famous for being a lovely white colour — 'pure white' as we say. When sunlight shines on it, it reflects it all back. For this reason we say sunlight is white light. When a rainbow is formed, sunlight is split up into the colours of the spectrum. White light is a mixture. A glass prism can split light up in similar fashion, and so can thin films, like soap bubbles, or a drop of oil on the surface of water. If white light can be split up into the rainbow colours, we should be able to make white light from them, and so we can. But it turns out that we do not need *all* the rainbow colours to do this. We need only red, green and blue. You can see this very thing happening when you watch colour television. In the introduction to some programmes, discs of red, green and blue are made to overlap, and you end up with the appearance shown in the picture. So we can say that the three primary colours of light are red, green and blue, and from these can be made yellow, magneta, turquoise — and white. And, indeed, other shades and hues by varying the strength and proportions of the primary colours.

But your experience with your paint box, as we have already mentioned, must surely be that you get green by mixing blue and yellow! This is true, but you are mixing *pigments*, not lights, in this case. If you think about what is happening to the white light that shines on your paints, you can understand it. Not every blue will make a good green when mixed with yellow. Cobalt blue is not as good as Prussian blue, is it? If you could examine the spectrum of the light reflected from a Prussian blue surface, you would see that it contained some green. So Prussian blue reflects blue and green from the white light that falls on it, but it *absorbs* red. Yellow absorbs blue, and reflects red and green. So when Prussian blue and yellow paints are mixed, all the mixture can reflect is green.

You can try further experiments by overlapping pieces of coloured paper such as are sometimes used for sweet wrappings. In the picture, which was made from three such discs overlapping, you can see how the system works. In the middle, where all three overlap, nothing is reflected, all is absorbed, so it appears black.

I used this information to help me once. I needed a large number of small coloured objects all the same size, in four distinct colours, for some counting work. I used rice grains, leaving some white, and staining some with red, and some with green food colouring. I made the black by staining with red AND green AND blue.

There is a lot of fun to be had with colour. How would you expect a pattern of red and white stripes to appear when viewed through (a) red and (b) green transparent film?

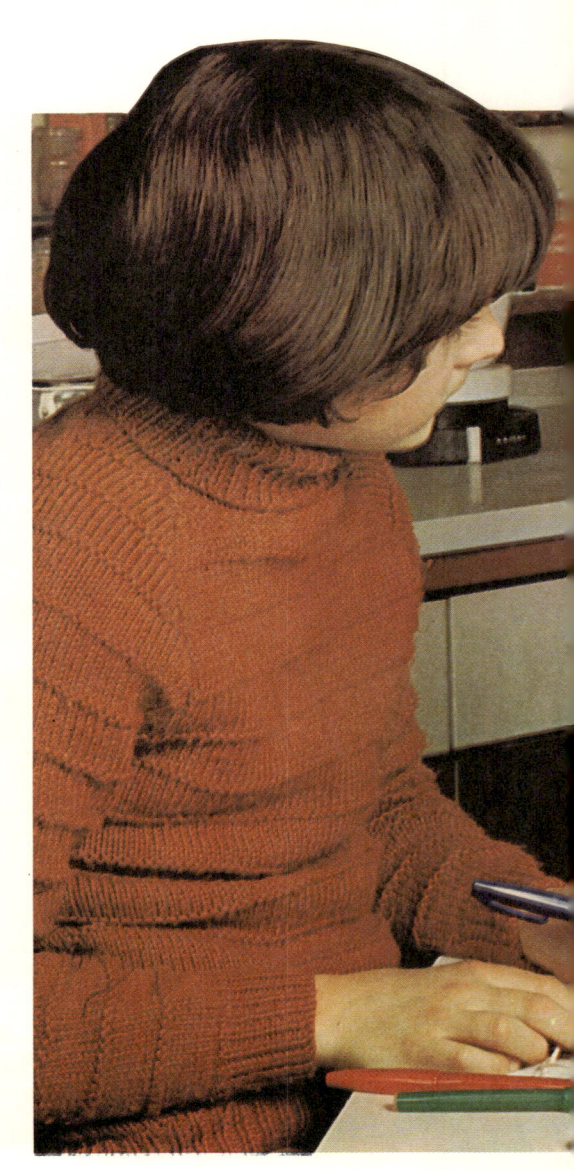

Above: here we have the effect of shining red, green and blue lights onto a white screen so that they overlap one another. This is true colour addition.

Above: the mixing of blue and yellow pigments to give green. The 'blue' absorbs (subtracts) red, and reflects blue and green. The yellow absorbs blue and reflects red and green. Both together reflect only green.

Above: when filters of turquoise, magenta and yellow overlap in pairs, they reflect only the common colour. All three together absorb everything and reflect nothing — hence the black. Compare the chromatography.

The pairs of colours in the three circles in the disc above are blurred together when the disc is spun (see the picture on the left). The lower disc shows the result you see when the disc is spinning rapidly. Does this agree with the top left picture on this page?

★ Fizz

> REMEMBER TO BLOW NOT SUCK. RINSE YOUR MOUTH IMMEDIATELY WITH PLENTY OF WATER IF YOU THINK YOU HAVE ACCIDENTALLY TAKEN IN LIME WATER. USE A SPOON WHEN HANDLING LIME.

You will remember from the white powder tests that one of the items, sodium bicarbonate, fizzed when vinegar was added to it. Bubbles appeared, too, in one of the jelly experiments using sodium bicarbonate and acid. The bubbles of gas in each case were of carbon dioxide. This is the gas that is formed when carbon burns in air. It combines with oxygen in so doing. This gas, carbon dioxide, is also formed in our bodies as a result of the special burning of our foods that goes on within us. There is a simple test for this gas. It gives a whitish, milky appearance to 'lime water'. This is not the drink made from lime fruit, but a solution (of calcium hydroxide) made by shaking garden or slaked lime with water. (Warning: do not handle, and take precautions against being splashed by this material.) You may need to strain or filter the solution to get the necessary clear lime water. If you breathe out gently, through a straw, into some lime water, you can test your own breath for carbon dioxide.

The pictures suggest a simple way of collecting gas, for testing, from things which fizz with water. Do you agree that it is carbon dioxide which comes from health salt? You can, if you collect larger samples of the gas, test whether carbon dioxide will let things burn in it. You can test your exhaled air in this way, too, and test whether your body has removed oxygen from the air you inhaled.

You will probably find carbon dioxide coming from most fizzing powders or tablets when you test them. But there is at least one interesting exception. The gas given off by tablets for cleaning false teeth will not change limewater, but it will relight smouldering string with a vengeance. The cleaning power of the tablet comes from this gas, which is OXYGEN.

a The solid is placed in the muslin, and kept in place over the funnel.
b A tube full of water is slipped over the tip of the funnel under water to collect the gas.
c The tube is corked before removing from the bowl for testing.

The Refrigerator

I had already used the refrigerator in the usual way in the jelly-making experiment. That is, I used it to keep things cool, to make a contrast with the comparative warmth of an ordinary room. This time the subject is the ice made by the refrigerator. It does this in two ways. Water placed in a container in the ice-making compartment freezes hard. Ice, as you will know, floats in water. It is less dense than liquid water, but as it is made of the same chemical substance, it presumably expands as it turns solid.

A good way of testing this is to take one of those metal tubes with a screw cap that encase cigars. Fill the tube quite full of water, and screw on the cap. This is best done whilst the tube is under water. Make sure there is no leakage, and put the tube of water in the ice-making compartment. Examine it some hours later. The picture shows what happened when I tried it. As the water froze, enough force was exerted as it expanded to split open the tube, and almost force the cap off.

Ice exerts a force as it expands on freezing. Would a compressing force make it melt, without heating? You can use a block of ice, made in a suitable container, to test this. Set the block of ice, as in the picture, with either end resting on a block of polystyrene (why?), and hang over it a *thin* wire (such as one strand from some multi-stranded electric flex) weighted down with some nuts or washers. The wire passes right through the block, yet leaves the ice still in one piece. The pressure of the wire does melt the ice; the wire sinks in the water formed; the next lot of ice below melts, but the water now above the wire, released from pressure, refreezes as it is still 'ice-cold'.

An ice skate makes a similar temporary melt, and slides on the temporary water lubrication, which refreezes as the skate moves on. If the temperature is a great deal below freezing point, as it may be in the Arctic, it may be too cold even for the compressed ice to turn to water, and skating becomes impossible.

But what is the second way in which the refrigerator makes ice? Every so often, a refrigerator has to be defrosted, because a great deal of ice collects around the coldest compartment, and takes up space. Where does this ice come from? The air in a room holds water vapour, and when this air comes in contact with the colder parts of the refrigerator, the water vapour condenses to liquid water which then freezes in the cold situation. This 'accidentally' formed ice can be very useful, for it is *nothing but* water, unlike tap water, which usually has minerals dissolved in it. (These sometimes form 'fur' in kettles. Test this fur with vinegar.) See too how films of water in trays in the freezing chamber produce interesting crystals of ice in minutes.

If you collect the water which forms as this ice melts on defrosting, you can use it as a substitute for rainwater for some of the experiments on living things we shall come to later.

These are, of course, only a few of the interesting things you can do with, and find out about ice. How can you discover how much of an iceberg shows above water? Some say one eighth, others one tenth. Do you agree with either? What difference does it make if the water in which it floats is (a) fresh or (b) salt?

The way the metal tube bursts as ice forms within it, shows what may happen when a water pipe freezes.

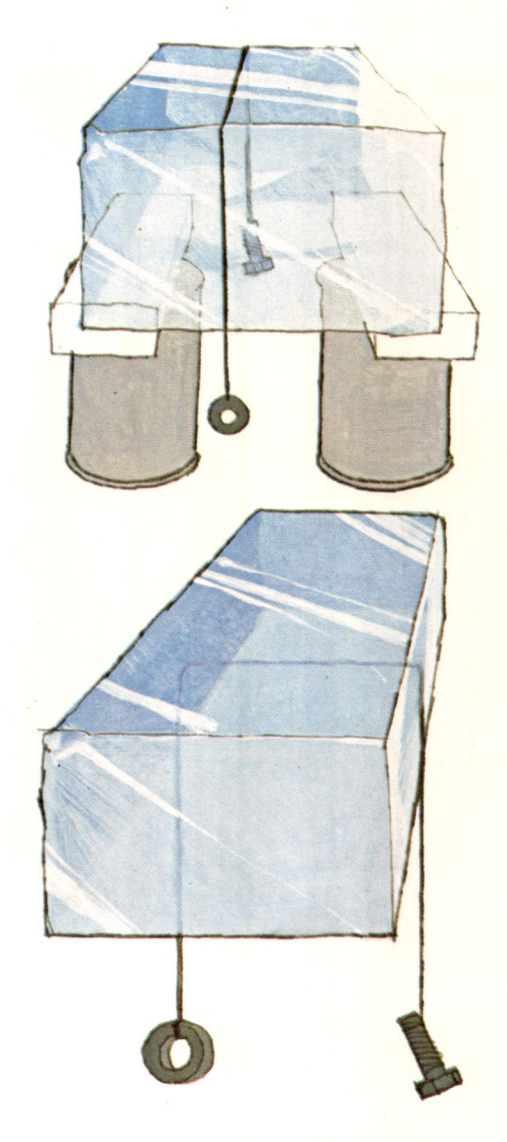

You could try different weights and different thicknesses of wire, and note differences in the time taken for the wire to pass through the ice. I think an interesting story could be written in which an arrangement like this was used as a timing device . . . 'the falling weight sprung the trap . . .'

★ Ways of Preserving

Foods can be preserved indefinitely in deep freeze, because the micro-organisms which, by feeding on foodstuffs, rot them and make them unfit for human use, cannot themselves live whilst frozen. What other ways of preserving are there? What we need are methods which keep the food fit to eat, and at the same time make it impossible for microbes to live on it.

I decided to test various methods using peas. From a packet of dried peas, I took three and put them in a clean glass tube — with a pinch of floor-dust to introduce microbes. I then screwed the cap on, and left the tube. I soaked a number of other peas in water, and put them, three at a time, each with a pinch of dust, in jars given the various treatments as in the picture. The one with just water and a pinch of dust was my 'control' which could be expected to produce rotten peas when kept at ordinary temperature. In a few days I got rotten peas. (Phew!) But three weeks later, all seemed to be well with the others. The one in the ice-making department remains frozen. I cannot actually can peas at home, but I boiled and sealed three of them with water. Of course, the dust cannot get at these, and any microbes already with them would have been killed by the boiling. I expected the brandy to have enough alcohol to poison the microbes, and the vinegar to be too acid for them to live in. The peas in the golden syrup shrivelled up, and look like dried peas again. This gives a clue to the way sugar preserves things, and tells why a well-made jam will keep. The sugar solution is so strong that water passes out from microbes (by 'osmosis') and they shrivel and cannot live.

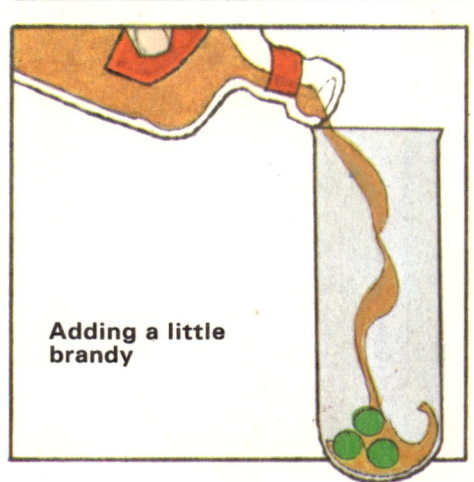

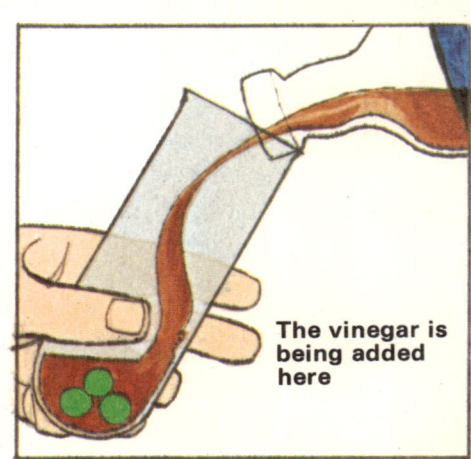

I do *not* in fact have a mammoth in the deep freeze, but a number of these huge extinct elephants have been found perfectly preserved in the ice of glaciers in Siberia, in which they doubtless became trapped accidentally.

Below are my preservation models. *I used an oven cloth for handling items in the heating method.*

Adding contaminating dust

Use the refrigerator for intense cold

Since this must be thoroughly heated you must take great care when fitting the lid or stopper

Adding the golden syrup

Adding a little brandy

The vinegar is being added here

Taming a Fungus

After some of my jelly preparations had been standing about for several days, a number of spots of mould began to grow on some of them. I had taken no steps to preserve them!

In fact, jelly preparations, usually on agar rather than gelatine, with suitable food mixes for various microbes, are regularly used for deliberately growing fungi (such as moulds) and bacteria. (I have already mentioned a similar use with *Marchantia*.) Mostly we see these fungi as nuisances, which destroy or at least spoil, some of our foods.

But we use some fungi and bacteria to do things we want. The vinegar we used as acid was mainly a solution of acetic acid, made by bacteria from alcohol. This had itself been made from sugar, by a fungus called yeast. From the sugar, yeast makes not only alcohol, but carbon dioxide too. It would not be easy for us to measure the alcohol made from sugar with home equipment, but we can attempt to do this for carbon dioxide.

To do this, we need a fairly thick, creamy mixture of flour and water. Measure equal amounts of this, say 25ml., into several cylindrical tubes. Meantime, prepare some yeast, either fresh from a baker, or from the dried variety. Measure different amounts, various eggspoonfuls, of active yeast, into the tubes, and different amounts of glucose sugar. The pictures show what happened in the few tubes I used in my trial. The swelling is due to carbon dioxide, bubbles of which are held by the sticky flour mix. What does the increase in size seem to depend on? What further experiments would you suggest to test your answer?

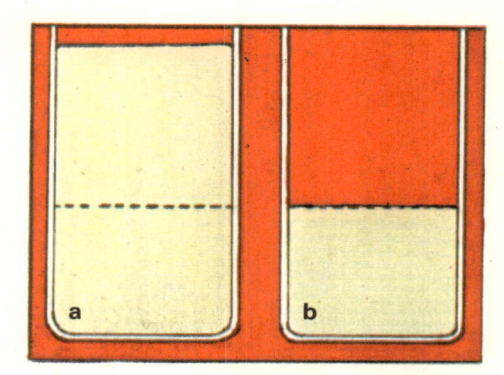

a 2 lots of glucose, 1 lot yeast
b No glucose. 1 lot yeast

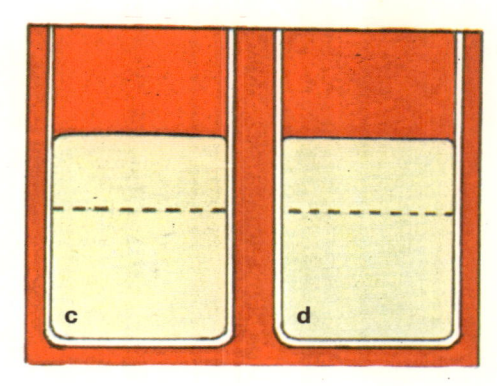

c 1 lot glucose, 1 lot yeast
d 1 lot glucose, 2 lots yeast

The dotted line in the pictures above shows the starting level in each case. You can see that the increase in volume varies with the amount of *one* of the items added. The apparatus we used is seen in the picture below.

Models

We have so far tried quite a number of different kinds of experiments. Another way in which scientists work is by using models. Here are some examples.

We are warm-blooded creatures. We keep a steady body temperature. How do we manage this? We can illustrate part of the answer by using a model. Take three containers, such as cans or plastic cups, of the same kind. Wrap one of them in a woollen garment, or a piece of fur. Put nothing around the other two. Put *equal* amounts of warm water – just hot enough to bear – in each of the three containers. Leave the wrapped one, and keep dabbing warm water on the *outside* of just *one* of the other two. After about 15 minutes, test the temperature of the water in all three containers. It is of course best to do this with a thermometer if possible, but even with a finger test, you should be able to agree that at the end, the wrapped one is warmest, and the moistened one coolest. The experiment models the way in which our clothes, or the fur of a mammal, or feathers of a bird keeps heat in, whilst moisture on the surface (sweating in life) has a cooling effect. Evaporating water takes heat from an object, whether container or living creature.

We can also set up a model to give a part answer to the question 'What use is skin?'. We cannot remove our own skin, but grapes have good skins which can easily be removed. I took four grapes of equal size and carefully skinned two of them, and then put skinned and unskinned in air and water as in the picture, and left them for several days. Try this yourself, for what happens teaches you about the value of skin better than my words would do.

But grapes are fruit, too. Let us consider some fruit.

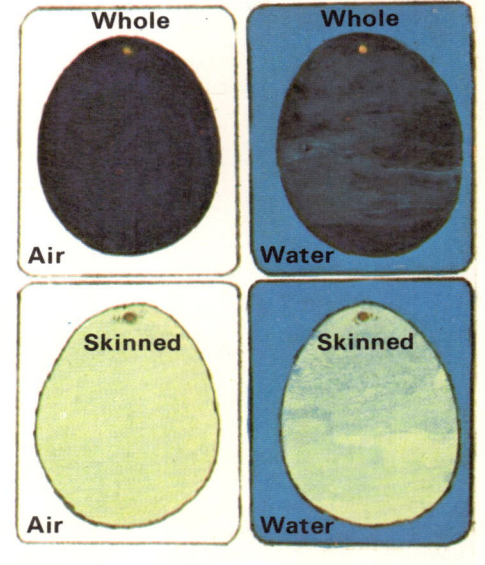

HERE IS A SIMPLE EXPERIMENT WHICH WILL GIVE YOU CLUES ABOUT THE VALUE OF YOUR SKIN.

Above: some people think birds have feathers just for flying, but they are at least as important for keeping warm. Most mammals have fur, but humans, being less hairy, need clothing to make up for this.

Left: look at the thermometers. You can see which of the vessels has lost most heat, though all started at the same temperature. You could take temperatures of all three at half minute intervals, from the start, and make an interesting graph of the results.

36

Hunt the Carpel

'It's as easy as shelling peas!' You may have heard someone say this about some task well within their powers. And, indeed, shelling peas is quite easy. But this is only so if you start on the usual, more curved, edge of the pod. It is not so easy to open along the straighter edge. If you do open a pod along this edge with great care, you will see that the opened pod is rather like a leaf, with the peas (i.e. seeds) arranged along its margin on either side. The name given to this leaf-like structure, with seeds along its margin, is a CARPEL. Most fruits are made of carpels, but they rarely look as much like leaves as they do in the pea plant. A pea or bean pod is just a single carpel, folded on itself to enclose the seeds in a seed box. But it is interesting to try to puzzle out the way in which carpels — often altered a good deal — make up other fruits. Each sector in an orange is a hairy carpel, and the hairs are so full of juice that they fill up the space within the sector. The pictures give you a number of examples of sections of familiar fruit, with diagrams to help you track down the carpels.

It is not always the case that the carpel wall makes the fruit, if by fruit we mean something juicy and nice to eat. In the case of the apple, for example, the carpels are sunk down into the support or receptacle which carries the flower. The part we eat is the juicy receptacle, and the carpel make up the core.

In a rose hip, the carpels are like little one-seeded nuts, attached to the inner wall of a receptacle shaped like a vase. The strawberry is a juicy mountain of a receptacle, and the 'seeds' on it are little, one-seeded nut-like structures, each from a single carpel.

In the banana, there are no seeds. At least the ones we can buy from the fruiterers in this country are seedless. I have eaten a banana with seeds in India, but only seedless varieties are grown commercially. If you examine the pulp of a banana carefully, you will see that it readily falls into three sections — each of these is a carpel, and little dots mark where the seeds would be.

Some 'fruits' aren't fruits at all. Rhubarb, which is made use of in tarts, and in jam, doesn't even look like a fruit — it looks like a stem. But it isn't a stem either. It is the juicy stalk of a leaf. The stem is a gnarled and woody item under the ground. Tomatoes *are* fruit, but are usually treated as 'vegetables'. We make a variety of uses of the various parts of plants, and it makes an interesting project to study the way plants are built, and to record the uses we make of them.

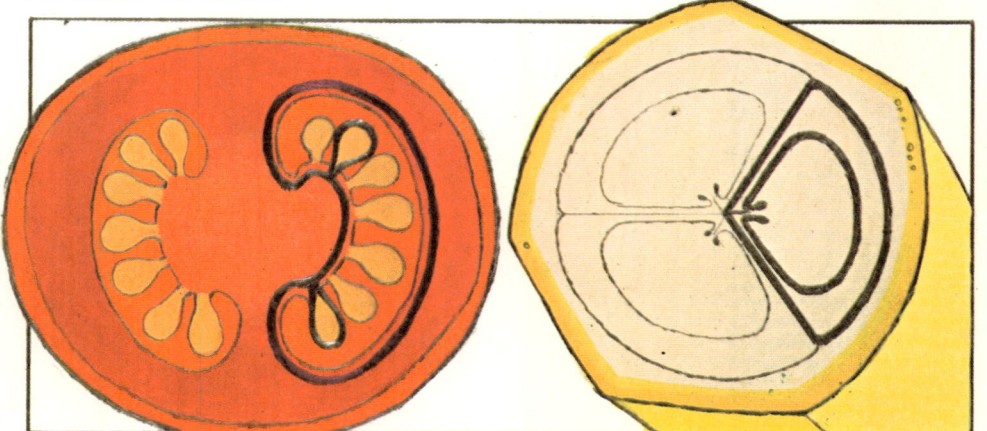

A Lucky Interlude

Having turned our attention to plants, let us go into the garden. Small though it is, a variety of plants grow in it. When I went out to choose items to write about I came across something quite unexpected.

Included among the flowers are roses and poppies. Some of the roses are single varieties, others are double. Poppies are almost always single, but I noticed that several of them seemed to have some smaller, extra petals. When I looked closely, I could see that some of these little petals seemed to have anthers on them, or perhaps one could say they were like stamens whose filaments had turned into petals.

The poppy and the rose have flowers with large numbers of stamens. Perhaps my unusual poppies give us a clue as to how such flowers as 'double' roses, which have many extra petals in addition to the five that single roses have, might have come into being. If in nature there are sometimes stamens which grow like petals, and we select, and breed and cross such plants, we may find we have plants which regularly have extra petals. There is reason to think that this happened in roses.

As I said, it was only by chance that I noticed these poppies. It pays to keep your eyes open for the unusual and unexpected. Nature sometimes tells its own stories.

This is a picture to remind you of the names of the flower parts we are talking about. It is interesting to see how these parts vary from flower to flower.

You can see how some of the smaller petals have anthers on them — or how some of the stamens are like petals! A normal poppy has four petals only.

A leaf covered with metal foil

Dropping the leaves in boiling water

Dissolving away the green chlorophyll

A Pictorial Interlude

When soaked in the iodine solution, the decolourised leaf goes blue — indicating the presence of starch.

We all depend on plants for food, directly or indirectly. Green plants can make sugar and starch from carbon dioxide and water, using their green chlorophyll, and the energy from sunlight. The starch is built up in the leaf during the day, and digested into sugar and sent elsewhere in the plant overnight. You can test this, in part, using information we already have.

If you completely cover a leaf with metal foil one afternoon, and then, about noon the next day, remove this leaf, and a normal one that you had not previously touched, you can test them for starch. One will have had sunlight that day, the other not. All you have to do is use the iodine test. The trouble is that the green colouring matter in the leaf hides the effect. So you must first get rid of the green chlorophyll. You could squash it out of the leaf, but that ruins the leaf. You know that methylated spirit will dissolve the chlorophyll. But this does not seem to work for a whole, living leaf. A leaf must first be killed with boiling water. Soaking in the spirit then removes the chlorophyll, leaving a pale leaf. Addition of iodine to the leaves in this condition should give you the blue colour, perhaps quite dark, in the sunlit leaf, showing there is starch there, but not in the other. The leaf must have light to make starch.

The pictures show how you can use a photographic negative to show that the amount of starch depends on the amount of light. Choose a healthy young leaf of not too coarse structure. You may have to try it a few times to get the right exposure for a print!

A starch-iodine blueprint from a leaf with a 'contrasty' negative clipped firmly over it, with a backing card to exclude light on the other side of the leaf.

How does your Garden Grow?

Though we value fruits as foods, it is the seeds that are important to the plants. We of course also eat many sorts of seeds. But what is a seed, and what does it need to start growing (i.e. germinate) and to keep on growing? You can easily answer the first question by opening and examining some larger seeds such as beans. The tiny young new plant is already there, with a food store and protective wrapping. It can rest like this for a long time.

We know that in moist, well prepared soil in the warmer spring and summer months seeds readily sprout. They are provided with warmth, moisture, air (in soil spaces), darkness, and the soil as such. You can test which of these conditions the seed really needs to germinate. For quicker results, it is best to use small seeds, such as mustard or cress. The pictures show how to set up a control, and a series of tests leaving out one condition at a time. I got good germination with the control, *and* with some of the others, showing that the leaving out of some of the conditions made no difference. But there was no germination when a certain set of three conditions were omitted. Which were these?

When I was planting some runner beans, I had a few seeds left over. They were of varying sizes. I decided to test the claim that small seeds germinate quickest. I trimmed one seed down to little more than the embryo, and cut a large seed down to the size of a small whole seed. I planted these together with a large seed. You can see from the picture the order in which they germinated. Their size after a fortnight gives a clue as to the value of the food store.

This experiment also suggests something interesting about natural history. If a squirrel, say, eats part of a seed, then drops it, so long as that seed still has its embryo intact, the seed may germinate and grow successfully — perhaps far from the parent plant.

What about growing on beyond germination? If you plant some seeds as shown in the picture, covering one with transparent plastic foil, and the other with light-excluding metal foil, you can compare growth in light and in dark. The light-grown ones were shorter, sturdy and well greened, the others straggly, not well developed, and yellow rather than green. A lot follows from this observation.

Here is an experiment to test the importance of water to plant growth. When you have a series of pots of seeds just germinating, give one pot no more water, give another two teaspoonfuls a day, give a third one teaspoonful every two days, and water a fourth quite heavily. What do you conclude about water and plant growth?

This next experiment, which shows how enormously important growing plants are, apart from their value as food, is one to attempt on a really bright sunny day. When plants make their carbohydrate from carbon dioxide and water, they also produce oxygen, which we need for breathing. We can use the 'fizz gas collection' apparatus here. 'Soda water' contains carbon dioxide in solution. The gas easily escapes from the water into the leaves.

The most important part of the seed — the embryo (shoot and root).

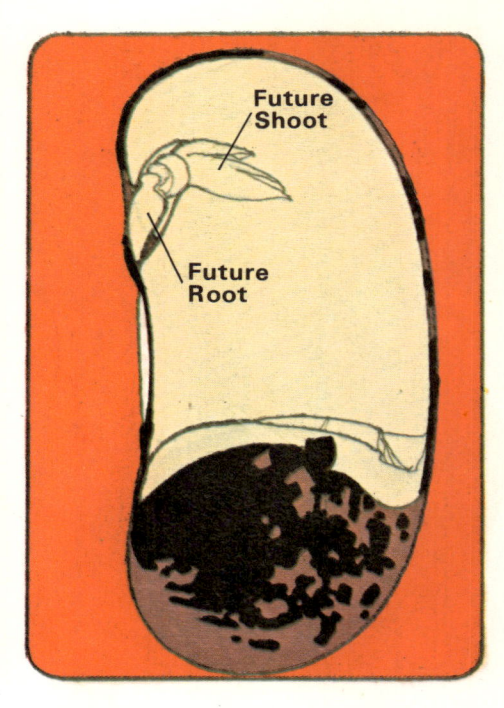

Below: the control is set up with seeds under moist loose soil in the warm. The other pots each leave out one factor at a time.

Seeds on surface — darkness replaced by light

a Embryo and very little food store
b Large seed cut down to size of (c)
c Small whole seed
d Large whole seed

The first seed up was (a) the small plant on the right, then followed (b) and (c) together (middle two). The last to appear was (d) on the left. The photograph was taken three weeks after planting. Though the smallest seed germinated first, in the long run the amount of food store made a great difference.

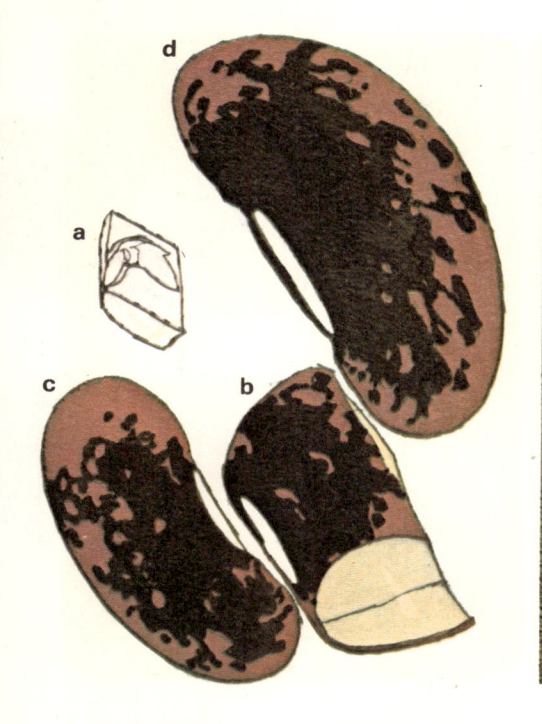

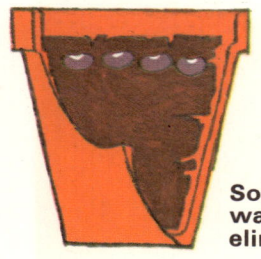

Soil quite dry – water eliminated

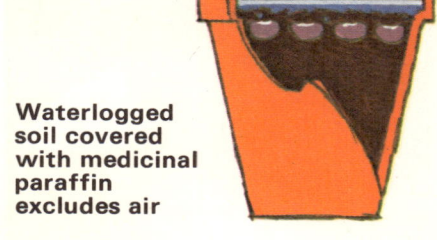

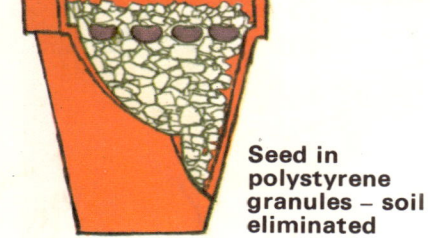

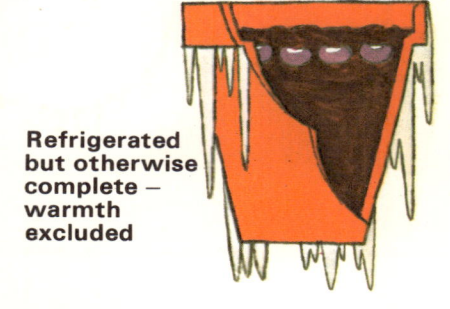

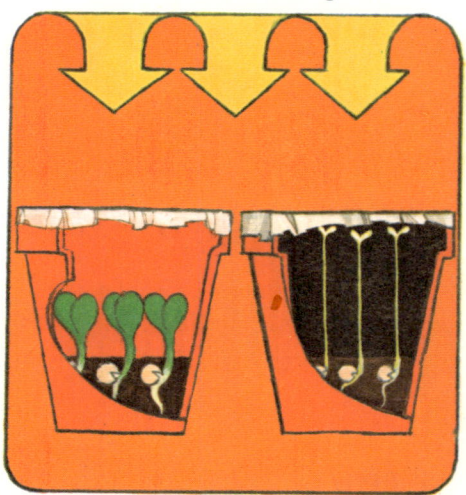

Waterlogged soil covered with medicinal paraffin excludes air

Seed in polystyrene granules – soil eliminated

Refrigerated but otherwise complete – warmth excluded

Direction of sunlight

The seeds **above left** were sown with a transparent cover, letting in light, above them. **Above right:** a cover of metal foil shuts out light. Short, green, sturdy plants grow in the light, pale and straggly ones in the dark. **Below:** 'before' and 'after' pictures of plants growing towards light from the side.

Bright sunlight

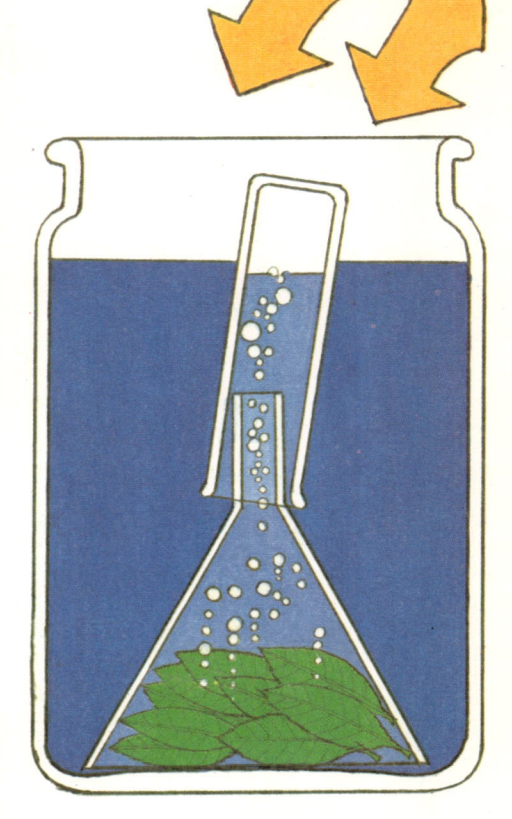

In setting up the apparatus **above** we need no muslin – which would in any case cut out light. Some soda water is added to the water to give extra carbon dioxide. The gas formed proves to be oxygen. This is a very important act by plants, providing us with the oxygen we need to breathe.

A Window-sill Mini Zoo

My garden grows animals as well as plants. It is frequently visited by cats and birds, but there is a permanent population of snails, earthworms, woodlice, ants, millipedes and spiders.

The earthworms, of course, live in the soil, and so do the ants. The woodlice are mainly to be found at the edge of a compost heap where it touches a concrete wall. But the other day I found some woodlice among a few damaged strawberries in my strawberry patch, which is several yards away from the compost heap. Did they, I wondered, prefer strawberries to their normal food of rotting vegetation?

To try to find this out, I prepared a tray of fine, moist soil, and put some squashed strawberries in one corner, and an equal amount of leaf, straw and wood from the compost heap in another corner. I collected about 20 woodlice, and kept them apart for a while, then put them in the tray as in the picture. I then covered the tray with a board to shut out light. After a while, I examined the tray and found most of the woodlice around and in the compost, but none near the strawberries. And so it was for several examinations. Then I removed all the compost, and replaced the cover. Later, when I examined the tray, most woodlice were at the strawberries.

This 'choice' experiment gives us the clue for finding out what conditions woodlice like. The pictures show some ways of testing choices. My experiments suggested that woodlice prefer dark, damp, cool places, with bits of rotting wood and vegetation. This amounts to a description of the conditions in which they live. So I set up a 'Zoo cage' for woodlice as in the picture.

The cover can be slid off to examine the woodlice. A north-facing windowsill is a good place for keeping this and other items of a mini-zoo.

Above: I find my woodlice prefer the top storey of their new home.

Here are some of the ways in which we can test woodlouse likes and dislikes. The cover has been taken off the 'strawberry and compost choice chamber for inspection **below**. Just to the right there are two tubes each of which has been half darkened by black paper. Woodlice are put in, straight into darkness in one, into the lit half in the other. **Far right:** a wet leaf/dry leaf choice test.

TRY TO FIND THE BEST CONDITIONS TO SUIT THE GARDEN CREATURES AND MAKE SURE YOUR ZOO SATISFIES THEM.

One of the most interesting of the features in this is sure to be the wormery. You may in fact want to set up several. The pictures suggest a simple way of setting them up, but there are a few tips to bear in mind. Use only soil that has been dug up with the worms, soil in which they were living. Let this soil dry, and sieve it, using the dry soil crumbs to build the layers of soil in the wormery. You can put in various materials as the 'sandwich filling' between two layers of soil. Sieved dried leaves are my 'standard' filling, but you could try such things as fresh chopped grass to see how worms take to them. Though the idea of the smaller jar within the jam jar is simply to force worms to use only a thin layer of soil, just within the glass of the jam jar, you can use the space within the smaller jar to house a 'control'. This is a small tube with exactly the same pattern of original layers put in it as the wormery itself. You have, with this control, something to compare throughout the existence of the wormery. If you use some of the refrigerator 'rainwater substitute' to keep the wormery moist, it can continue literally for years. As time goes on you will need to supply bits of leaf at the surface as food for the worms. You can make use of this to test whether there are preferences for sorts — or shapes — of leaf offered.

The ant colony is the least easy to set up, for at least one queen needs to be present for a thriving colony. But it is worth trying. Stand the 'cage' in a tray, surrounded as you see by a moat of water containing detergent. Why the moat, and why the detergent?

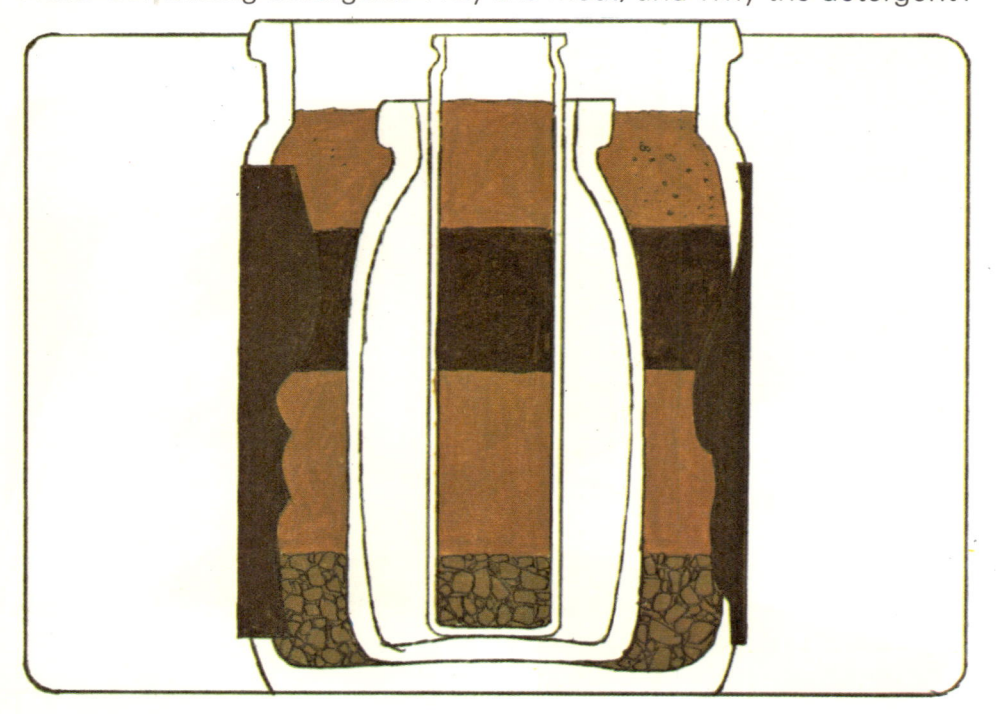

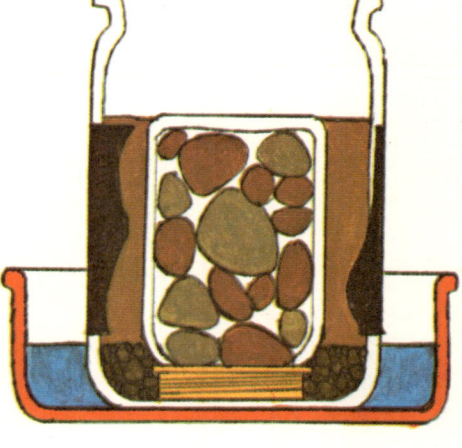

The ant colony above has a smaller jamjar with lid and is upside down inside a larger jar. The pebbles in it keep it steady whilst soil is put in between it and the larger jar. The base of the jamjar makes a platform for food, and the bowl contains water with detergent. The water alone would not wet the shiny surface of ants that tried to wander away.

To the left is a section through a wormery that has been set up for a little while. It is interesting to note, in the early stages, which materials the worms seem to occupy, to eat or to avoid. Later on you can see the way worms mix up and drain the soil.

Further Tasks

We have by no means dealt completely with the things we could investigate about the house. It would take a very big book indeed to get anywhere near that, and it would even then be incomplete.

In the remaining space, I want to mention some of the other things that might have started off investigations. You might like to follow up a few of them yourselves. For there is the Case of the Obstinate Custard Powder. The instructions on the packet direct the cook to mix the powder to a paste or cream with a little cold milk, before pouring on boiling milk. But as you mix the paste, you find you can only do it slowly. The paste flows easily, and drips off the spoon. But if you try to stir quickly, it siezes up, and even *cracks* as if it were brittle. The explanation for this would take us into a discussion of viscosity and cohesion — which would be very technical. But we could very well have compared the behaviour of various thick liquids, such as syrup — or non-drip paint. The latter does not flow or drip of its own accord, but flows easily when stirred. This is quite the reverse of the custard!

What is it that happens when things are cooked? Why do things look, smell and taste different when boiled rather than baked? If you take exactly the same scone mix and cook it on a hot plate, do you get the same result as if you cook it under a grill — or in the oven? How much can recipes be varied, and still produce products fit to eat? There is food for thought, at least, in these questions.

We might have continued a study on solution. What materials dissolve in what liquids (solvents) and what different amounts of materials can a given solvent take into solution? I warn you of a surprise if you try this with sugar and water.

I mentioned the link between gelatine and glue. There are many sorts of glue to be had these days. Which glues are best for sticking particular materials together? It would be very useful to do experiments to find out which glues NOT to use with some materials. To hope to mend a plastic toy, and find that the glue you use just dissolves it away, can be very upsetting.

The stones in my garden are mainly flint. But if you have a variety of them, you could start a study of petrology (as the study of rocks is called). Find out which stone scratches which, and put them in a hardness league, with top scratcher as the leader, and the softest, which can be scratched by all the others, but itself scratches none, at the bottom of the class. Include glass as a 'rock' if you do this.

A casual observation by some young friends of mine makes yet another starting point. The tiny sweets known as 'hundreds and thousands' in a clear transparent plastic tube sometimes dance about when the tube is handled. When the tube is rubbed vigorously on a woollen garment, especially in cold dry weather, they can dance wildly. The little 'silver balls' used for decorating cakes, in similar plastic tubes can also behave in an interesting way. Try it! This starts you off on the study of electrostatics.

But I have no doubt that the best and most interesting investigations will come from your very own observations and questions. Keep your eyes open, ask the right questions, and you will make the *experiments* give you the answers.

The brittle custard. You can use water instead of milk.

A lump of dough baked and a lump of dough boiled!

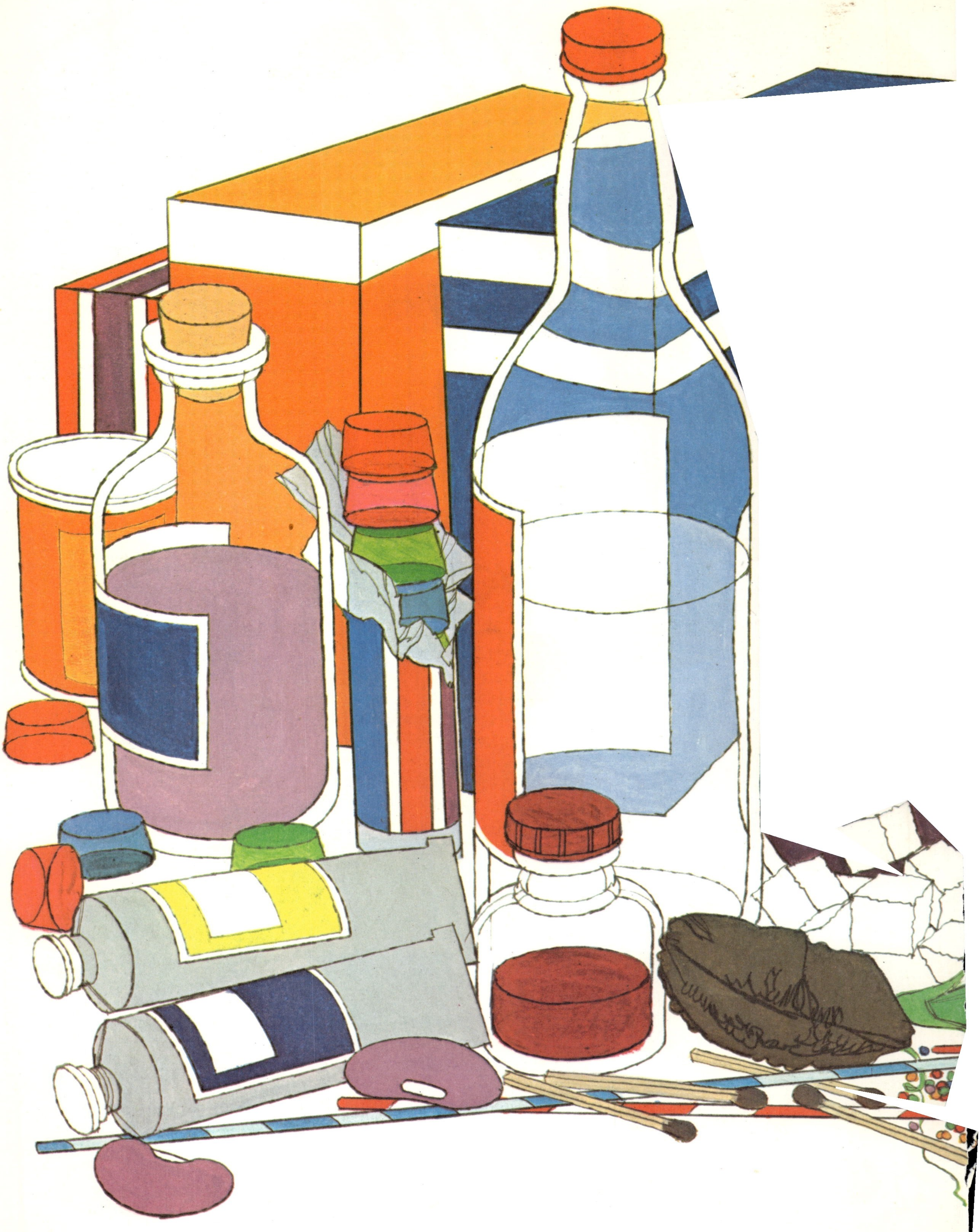

Preparing to test the way in which various things dissolve.

What sticks to what best? There are many different adhesives to try.

Collect a good variety of stones before trying the scratch test.

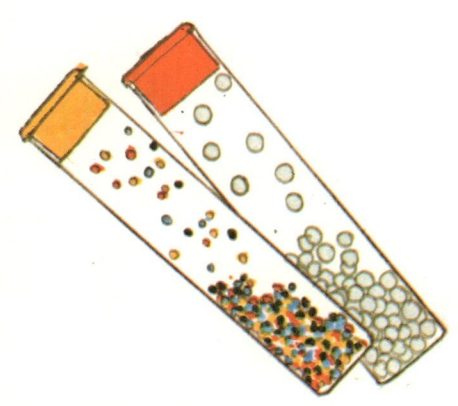

Do not fill the tubes – dancing dots need room to move!

Onwards

Here we are at the end of the book. But you will not want it to be the end of your interest in science. We have had examples of observations leading to questions, and of questions leading to experiments which we hoped would give us answers. Often these answers led to further questions.

In the experiments we have had examples of using a 'control' with which to compare the different 'treatments' we used. In some of these treatments, we varied the amounts of material used. This use of measured amounts is important in science.

We have touched on some of the main branches of science. Where we dealt with heat, and light (colour) and force (as in the melting and freezing ice) we were in the field of PHYSICS – the science of energy. The burning and fizzing and talk of acids and alkalis were examples of CHEMISTRY – the science of matter and its changes. The living things – plants, small animals, and ourselves, are the subject matter of BIOLOGY – the science which deals with life. The few experiments on enzymes dealt with part of the chemistry of life – Biochemistry.

A scientist spends a good deal of his time reading what other scientists have done, and found out, and what their ideas are. There is a great deal for you to read in the future about science. You could take your next step with 'My World of Science' and the 'Junior Science Encyclopedia'. Your teachers at school, and the librarian at your local library will be able to help you greatly with further reading.

Have an enjoyable time with science, about the house, and in the world at large.